Mongolia

Mongolia

Photography
Olaf Meinhardt

Text
Achill Moser

BUCHER

Contents

Mountain range near Ulaan Uul: Paradise for those seeking solitude.

Watching livestock with binoculars in northern Mongolia.

In Erdene Zuu monastery.

A glacier in the Altai Mountains.

Sand dunes sculpted by the wind in the Gobi Desert.

Splendid gates of honor lead into the monastery of Dunhuang.

Traveling with a folding canoe.

The north of Mongolia with the grandiose Darchad Valley is the habitat of nomadic Mongols. Milking their herds is an everyday task for the nomads. From summer to fall a mare will be milked several times. The Mongols use the fermented milk to make a slightly alcoholic beverage known as "airag."

The mountains seem to stand on their heads in the glassy-smooth water of the Tuul Gol.

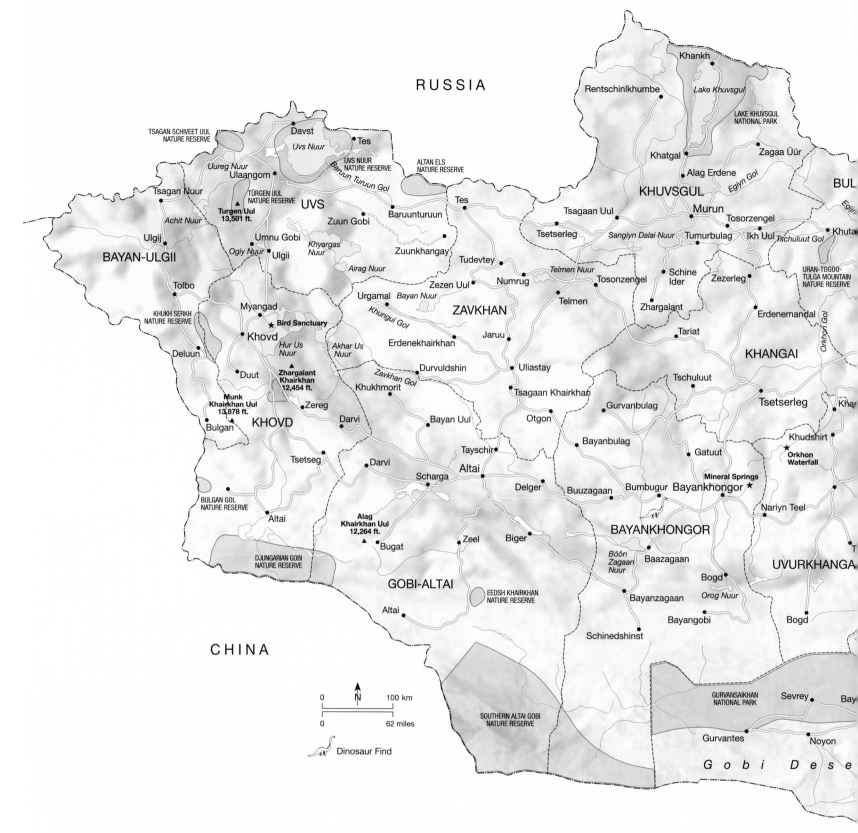

RUSSIA

TSAGAN SCHIVEET UUL NATURE RESERVE

Davst
Uvs Nuur
Tes

UVS NUUR NATURE RESERVE

ALTAN ELS NATURE RESERVE

Uureg Nuur
Ulaangom
Tsagan Nuur

TÜRGEN UUL NATURE RESERVE
▲ Turgen Uul 13,501 ft.
UVS
Zuun Gobi

Baruunturuun

Tes

Achit Nuur

Umnu Gobi
Ogiy Nuur
Ulgii

Khyargas Nuur

Zuunkhangay

Tudevtey

Ulgij

BAYAN-ULGII

Airag Nuur
Zezen Uul
Numrug

Tolbo

Urgamal
Bayan Nuur

ZAVKHAN

Myangad
★ Bird Sanctuary
Khovd

Khungui Gol

Jaruu

KHUKH SERKH NATURE RESERVE

Deluun

Hur Us Nuur
Akhar Us Nuur

Erdenekhairkhan

Durvuldshin

Uliastay

Duut
▲ Zhargalant Khairkhan 12,454 ft.
Khukhmorit

Zavkhan Gol

Tsagaan Khairkhan

Munk Khairkhan Uul 13,878 ft.
Zereg

Darvi

Bayan Uul

Otgon

KHOVD

Bulgan

Tsetseg

Darvi

Tayschir
Altai

Scharga
Altai

Delger

Buuzagaan

BULGAN GOL NATURE RESERVE

Altai

Alag Khairkhan Uul 12,264 ft.

DJUNGARIAN GOBI NATURE RESERVE

▲ Bugat

Zeel

Biger

Bumbugur
Bayankhongor
★ Mineral Springs

Bayanbulag

BAYANKHONGOR

GOBI-ALTAI

EEDSH KHAIRKHAN NATURE RESERVE

Böön Zagaan Nuur
Baazagaan

Altai

Bayanzagaan

Schinedshinst

KHUVSGUL

Khankh
Rentschinlkhumbe
Lake Khuvsgul

LAKE KHUVSGUL NATIONAL PARK

Khatgal
Zagaa Üür
Alag Erdene

Tsagaan Uul
Murun
Tosorzengel

Tsetserleg

Egiyn Gol

Sangiyn Dalai Nuur
Tumurbulag
Ikh Uul
Tschuluut Gol

Telmen Nuur
Tosonzengel
Schine Ider
Zezerleg

BUL

Egiin

Khuta

URAN-TOGOO-TULGA MOUNTAIN NATURE RESERVE

Telmen

Zhargalant

Erdenemandal

Orkhon Gol

Tariat

KHANGAI

Tschuluut

Gurvanbulag

Tsetserleg

Khar

Khudshirt
★ Orkhon Waterfall

Gatuut

Nariyn Teel

UVURKHANGA

Bogd

Orog Nuur

Bayangobi
Bogd

GURVANSAIKHAN NATIONAL PARK
Sevrey
Bay

SOUTHERN ALTAI GOBI NATURE RESERVE

Gurvantes
Noyon

Gobi Dese

CHINA

0   100 km
N
0   62 miles

🦕 Dinosaur Find

"Our relationship with nature is simply different. A mountain is a mountain, and when I sit on this mountain, then I consist of stone and peace. I have no other task. And when I walk across the steppe, then I am grass; I feel myself growing or withering; I smell my scent or hear myself rustling. And when I wade through a river, then I am water; I am flowing. I can also transfer this thought to other objects. Sometimes I am a glacier, sometimes a tree, sometimes air; always I am a part of the earth and of the sky and of all that is in between."

In the Land of the Angry Winds, Galsan Tschinag and Amélie Schenk

RUSSIA

Kyakhta
chig Sukhbaatar
Schaamar
Khuder
ge Murun
Orkhon Gol
Darkhan
Bugant
SELENGE
Orkhon
Scharyngol
Baruunkharaa
khontuul
Zhargalant
Batsumber
Bayantschandmani
GORKHI-TERELDSH
NATURE RESERVE
Ulan Bator
Baganuur
KHUSTAYN UUL
NATURE RESERVE Nalaykh
Lun
Bayan
Erdenesant
Tuul Gol
CENTRAL AIMAQ
Buren
Bayan
Undshuul
Adaatsag
an Undur
Erdenedalay
Delgertsogt
Mandal Gobi
han Ovoo
MIDDLE GOBI Undurschil
Uldsiit
Zogt Ovoo
Manlay
Tsogt Tsetsi
Dalandsadgad
Khanbogd
Bayan Ovoo
SOUTHERN GOBI

Verkhniy
Ul'Khun
Bayandun
Dadal
Bayan Uul
Norovlin
Batschireet
Binder
Bayan
Adraga
KHENTII
Batnorov
Berkh
Bayan
Ovoo
Undurkhaan
Bayanmunk
Darkhan
Galskhar
Tskhoyr
Ikh Khet
Ayrag
EAST GOBI
Mandakh
Saynshand
Zuunbayan
Erdene
Ulaan
Badrakh
Khuvsgul
Khatanbulag

HAN HENTEYN
NATURE RESERVE

MONGOL DARIGANGA
NATURE RESERVE
Ereenzav
UGTAM
NATURE RESERVE
CHINA
Wall of Genghis Kahn
Bayantal
Khalkhgol
Tschoybalsan
Buir
Nuur
Sumber
Yirxie
Kherlen Gol
DORNOD
NUMRUG
NATURE RESERVE
EASTERN MONGOLIA
NATURE RESERVE
Munkkhaan
Baruun Urt
Matad
SUKHBAATAR
LATSCHINVANDAD UUL
NATURE RESERVE
Tuvschinschiree
Erdenezagaan
Dariganga
GANGA NUUR
NATURE RESERVE
Naran
CHINA

INNER MONGOLIA

Ar Saynshand
Zamyn Uud

CHINA

Gobi Desert

A magical charm emanates from the **Gobi,** the largest desert region of Central Asia. The nomads have learnt how to live in this inhospitable region.

The sky dominates the striking and lonely landscapes of the **Khangai Mountains**. In the heartlands of Mongolia there are peaks rising to heights of 2,600 to 3,400 meters (8,528–11,152 feet). Numerous streams and rivers have carved their way deep into the mountains and pour their waters into the Orkhon and the Selenge rivers, finally flowing into Lake Baikal.

The Home of Genghis Khan's Heirs

The Mongolian Steppe is wide as the ocean. It stretches from the Siberian taiga in the north to the stone and sand deserts of the Gobi, and from the "Great Lakes Basin" in the west to the Great Wall of China in the east. The country of the descendants of Genghis Khan is above all one of wide open spaces, a fascinating expanse over which the wind blows unceasingly. It combs the high grass of the steppe; it drives whirling banners of sand through desolate valleys; it curls the surface of the huge lakes and whistles round the mountain passes of the high peaks; and all the while the clouds form their ever-changing fantasy shapes against a sky of the deepest blue.

That is why the old Mongols knew that their land was inhabited by whole hosts of invisible gods, spirits and demons.

Mongolia is almost four times the size of the United Kingdom and twice as large as Texas – a land of endless dimensions where all subjects and objects, such as animals and yurts, are nothing more than tiny dots on the horizon. And every object, and most especially the appearance of a person, becomes a minute but unmistakable sensation in this seemingly abandoned emptiness.

The traveler here will also experience the most insignificant occurrence – the whirling of the sand, a stone rolling along, or the grass swaying in the wind – as an event of almost biblical proportions.

Mongolia, even at the beginning of the 21st century, is still a largely unknown country, a "terra incognita." Here the traveler can experience a land far removed from the everyday world and full of archaic scenery and fantastic landscapes, in which nature

In the unspoiled nature of the Altai Mountains, cyclists have fantastic opportunities to set up camp, surrounded by the majestic wilderness. – In the Altai Mountains at Khoton Nuur, where the nomads of the steppe find sufficient pasture-land and water for their herds, the Mongols occasionally set up their yurts (right-hand page).

In the lush, green Darkhad Valley of northern Mongolia, where the nomads erect their yurts, life is good to the Mongolians who often seem happy and contented. – Kazakhs, who are at home in the High Altai, are normally seen in their typical black coats. Even today, they still train eagles for hunting.

presents itself in manifold shapes and colors. This is the home of silence, and of raging storms which uncover from time to time the geological testimony to millions of years of history, a testimony that can be observed in many places.

As early as the Stone Age, small groups of hunters and reindeer herders dwelt in the high steppe surrounded by mountains. The cold, dry climate forced them to lead a nomadic existence, surviving by hunting and raising livestock. In succeeding periods, the wide steppe and mountain massifs of present-day Mongolia remained a political vacuum until the 7th century AD.

Turkic-Mongolian clans who lived as nomadic herders in this region were known as "Barbarians" by their Chinese contemporaries. Not until the 11th century did many of these nomadic families join together to form small, independent nations that now and again undertook military campaigns against each other. The Kyrgyz in the Mongolian Highlands were driven back northwards,

14

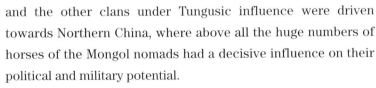

and the other clans under Tungusic influence were driven towards Northern China, where above all the huge numbers of horses of the Mongol nomads had a decisive influence on their political and military potential.

About the Origins of the First Mongol Princes

Even in very early times, the Chinese feared the constantly growing urge for expansion of the wild peoples from the steppe. They therefore tried to hold back the Mongolian and Turkic tribes with ramparts and walls. But when the Chinese Tang dynasty broke apart in the 10th century as the result of an uprising, the nomadic peoples of the Mongolian Steppe gained more and more strength. In their hostile environment, they had learned to live an ascetic life that was shaped primarily by tribal feuds, hunting and a religious awe of nature.

Home of the Camel and the Snow Leopard

Wild camels and snow leopards in Mongolia have long been protected from hunters. Nevertheless, the numbers of these species continue to decline. The two-humped wild camel (Bactrian camel) is now almost only found in Central Mongolia. The havtagai camels, as the Mongols call them, have been used too intensively as a domestic animal and beast of burden. They are tenacious animals that even with a load of 150 kilograms on their backs can cover a distance of 50 kilometers a day.

Mongolia – with resources of around 600,000 animals – is one of the world's leaders in camel-raising. Two-thirds of the animals live in the desert steppe of the Gobi, where the population carries out intensive camel breeding. Besides fresh milk, various other milk products and meat, camel hair is also an important product. This means the Bactrian camel is a fully adequate alternative to cattle-raising.

Even rarer than the wild camel is the snow leopard (irbis), one of the big cats, It has yellow-grey fur and is equally at home in the eternal snows of the Gobi-Altai Mountains or in the steppes of the desert. The number of free-roaming snow leopards, which catch their prey (rodents, ibex and wild sheep) with an ambush-like jump, is estimated today at a mere fifty animals.

It is the great annals of the Chinese Empire that provide us with the most detailed source material regarding the extraction of the first of the Mongol princes, who are descended from the mythical kings of Tibet. These annals also relate the story of Yesugei Baghatur, who once encountered a Tatar tribe while out hunting mountain hares with his brother.

He kidnapped a girl from this tribe, Hoelun, and married her. In the year 1162 she bore him a son who was named Temüjin. Brought up in the traditions of the peoples of the steppe, at the age of 13, Temüjin witnessed his father being poisoned during a feast by his Tatar relations.

From then on, Temüjin was brought up by his mother. He learnt all the skills of the military arts, and in the end was a better horseman and warrior and could use a bow and arrow more skillfully than any other member of his tribe.

Soon Temüjin was the leader of a band of robbers and, as their leader, he killed his hostile relatives before taking up the struggle, supported by his Mongolian hordes, against his arch-enemies – the Tatars.

In the fall of the year 1206, Temüjin summoned all his tribal princes to a gathering in the grasslands of the River Kerulan, where he proclaimed himself Khan. One of the old chronicles relates in this instance, "Starting that day, a colorful bird in the form of a lark settled on a square stone in front of the house three

mornings in succession and cried 'Genghis, Genghis!' That is how Temüjin received the name Sutu Bogda Genghis Khan, by which he became renowned in all regions."

The Most Illustrious Era

Under the supreme command of Genghis Khan, who united the clans and tribes that had previously been divided by ancient feuds, the Mongol people enjoyed their most illustrious era. Genghis Khan abolished the old social order based on genealogical hierarchy, introduced new divisions of the society of the steppe and passed new laws that he had chiseled in stone throughout the land, so that they were visible to everyone. And moreover, no bulwark could resist the Mongolian horde with its war cry, "One sun in the heavens, one ruler on the earth."

With the insignias of their power, nine standards made of white horsehair, the Mongols swarmed out on their shaggy horses across Asia and Europe. They subdued the Kyrgyz and Oirat tribes, invaded Northern China in 1211 and four years later conquered Beijing. In 1219, Genghis Khan took an army of

Inside a yurt, a Kazakh girl plays a traditional plucked instrument, the domra (large photograph). People in the Altai Mountains wear ornate rings and beautifully decorated belts (left and below). Older people are shown great respect, as the wisdom of older people is highly esteemed (left-hand page).

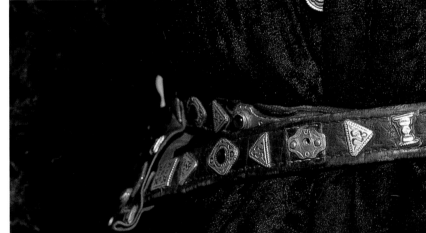

200,000 soldiers to Central Asia and in 1223 he defeated the Russian army at Taganrog in the Battle of the Kalka River.

In 1227, the Mongol ruler died at the age of 72, after receiving a serious wound in a punitive campaign against the Western Xia (Tanguts).

His successor and the supreme commander of the Mongol Empire was his third son, Ögödei, who continued the campaign against China, while Batu, a grandson of Genghis Khan, conquered Russia and Poland and in 1241 defeated the army of German-Polish knights near Liegnitz. The equestrian armies of the Mongols even occupied Hungary and were close to Wiener-Neustadt (near Vienna), when they suddenly stopped short and returned to their original homeland, where their Great Khan Ögödei had died.

At least one million Mongols had succeeded, then, in conquering an area of around 25 million square kilometers (9.65 million square miles), with the same number of inhabitants. It was the largest empire in the world in its time, and it increased trade, traffic, and cultural exchange along the trans-Asian routes with a dynamic effect that lasted almost two hundred years.

The Fall of the Vast Mongol Empire

After the death of Ögödei, the first weaknesses in the Mongol Empire became apparent. Intrigues and family quarrels led to its disintegration, after which it reformed as a number of independent states. Even Kublai Khan, who was proclaimed Great Khan in the year 1264, did not succeed in regaining supremacy of the continent of Asia. Instead, he continued with the conquest of all of China, and in the process he transferred the capital of the Mongols from Kharakhorum to Shang-tu near Dolonor, and later to Beijing.

In the year 1271, Kublai Khan assumed the title of Emperor of China and founded the Yuan Dynasty (1271–1368). During this era, the early feudal Mongol Empire had its heyday. It was the largest coherent state that ever existed on the Asian continent, even though the rule of the Mongols increasingly took on Chinese forms.

After the death of Kublai Khan in the year 1294, Iran and large parts of Russia fell away from the Mongol federation. Togoontömör Khan took over as ruler. But his extravagant lifestyle and

See page 23

17

Equestrian Prince and King of the Steppe:

Genghis Khan

1 Picture of the renowned Genghis Khan (about 1155–1227), the founder of the Mongol Empire. – 2 Genghis Khan pronounces a judgment (Persian book illustration from the 14th century). 3 Genghis Khan in the pulpit of the mosque of Bukhara (Persian miniature, around 1397/98).

In a time when virtually everyone was fighting against everyone, and the ruling power could barely maintain its position for more than three generations in the context of a large empire, "Temüjin" (he who works with iron), whose name means something like "smith," was born in the middle of the seventh decade of the 12th century. In those days, the Mongol people was still largely known by the name "Dada." It was politically, economically and socially close to collapse, despite having achieved a certain measure of power in the early 12th century under the leadership of Khabul Khan.

Born into an aristocratic family descended from nomadic herders, Temüjin lost his father at a young age, when his tribe, which lived in the northeast of present-day Mongolia between the Kherlen and Onon rivers, was attacked by enemies. Temüjin himself, who even then was already a robber and horse thief and who as a youth had experienced all the adversity of an environment that by Central Asian standards was desolate, was taken captive.

He escaped by means of a adventurous flight that won him great admiration and loyal followers. With their support, he soon had his first success in warfare, before suffering a severe defeat in the decisive battle near Dalan Baljut against his rival Jamuqa, who had earlier been his blood brother.

For almost a decade, Temüjin was forced to remain outside the country. Presumably he found refuge with the Jurchens who ruled northern China as the Jin Dynasty from 1115 to 1234. Temüjin returned in 1195 to take up the struggle against the Tatars, as leader of a fighting force of 100 men. Gradually, and with unrelenting harshness, he succeeded in eliminating all his rivals.

According to the motto "If heaven is merciful, then it will succeed," the hordes of the Mongolian cavalry overran all the great nation-cultures of that period in the following years, and in 1206 Temüjin completed the full unification of the nomadic Mongol tribes. He finally succeeded in settling their bloody feuds and, within three decades, in founding an empire of hitherto unknown dimensions, stretching from the Caspian Sea to the Pacific Ocean.

At the same time, Temüjin had himself proclaimed Genghis Khan, the supreme ruler of all Mongols – Genghis being a word of Turkish origin meaning "ocean." It is a term which is closely related to the wide expanses of Mongolia.

The condition for this enormous excess of power was the founding

3

of a unified Mongolian state in the form of a strictly ruled monarchy based on violence and oppression. Temüjin also altered the founding principles of Mongolian society.

It was no longer background, origin, and rank that determined the respect and position of a Mongol, but personal attitudes, performance and individual achievements. In addition, there was a functioning state system and a well organized and equipped cavalry that defeated every army that opposed the Mongols between North China and Persia.

Genghis Khan led his final campaign in 1227 in the Gobi Desert, against the Western Xia (Tanguts). Whether it was during this campaign, or on a later hunting expedition, that he received such a severe injury that he died soon afterward, has never been finally determined. His last resting place is also unknown.

In the Altai Mountains.

the excessive striving for power by some of the mighty princes led to conspiracies, revolts, and fratricidal warfare that ultimately marked the beginning of the decline of the vast empire.

Finally, in the year 1368, the entire Chinese people stormed the capital city, Beijing, overthrew the Yuan Dynasty and liberated itself from Mongolian rule. Togoontömör Khan fled back to Mongolia with his followers – to Kharakhorum.

After the latter's death, the last Russian Grand Duke broke away from the empire, and Mongolia split up into a number of federated states. Some of the princes attempted to re-conquer the lost regions, but they did not have the strength to withstand the Chinese armies. All efforts to reunite the feuding tribes under a common ruler were equally fruitless.

Not until the early 16th century did Dayan Khan achieve this – for the last time, however. For when he died in the year 1543, there were renewed signs of fragmentation among the various ethnic groups. The situation was exploited by the fast-growing Manchurian Empire in China. Over a period of 150 years, they conquered the Mongol Empire, by force of arms and by deception.

First, southern Mongolia was forced to acknowledge Manchu rule in 1636, before – one year later – the subjection of northern Mongolia took place. The latter region is approximately equivalent to that of present-day Mongolia.

Seven Hundred Monasteries are Founded in the Steppe

Alongside valuable merchandise, a large variety of different beliefs entered the area of present-day Mongolia during that period, along the numerous routes of the Silk Road. These included Manichaeism and Nestorianism from the Byzantine Empire, Zoroastrianism from Persia, and Islam from Arabia. But it was primarily Lamaism, a branch of Buddhism from India and Tibet, that in the 15th and 16th centuries replaced the shamanism which had previously been widespread among the nomads of Mongolia.

These new beliefs gave the Mongolians who inhabited the steppe an effective way of protecting themselves from natural and supernatural dangers. They were also influenced by the numerous festivals that were celebrated annually in honor of the countless Buddhist gods, as well as the typical rituals involving with prayer wheels, drums, banners and mysterious dances.

In the most remote areas of the Mongolian Altai, unpaved dirt roads lead through the endless grass steppe where numerous mountain streams meander, and sometimes whole herds of horses roam freely along their banks.

Eventually, the teaching of the Lamaist-Buddhist religion on the migration and salvation of the soul dominated the entire Central Asian steppe. More than 700 monasteries were constructed. The main monastery was founded in the valley of the Tuul in the southern part of the Khentii Mountains and formed the core of the monastic city of Urga, which was gradually developing at that time.

In addition, Lamaism was transforming the warlike spirit of the Mongols. The productive powers in Mongolia stagnated as more followers subscribed to the "Yellow Hat Order" of Tsongkhapa (1356–1418), who had derived Lamaism from the Buddhist teaching of salvation in the Tibetan monastery of Gandan. As the previously bold horsemen and warriors adopted a celibate lifestyle, the natural growth of the clans was progressively diminished.

It was the teaching of Mongol-Tibetan Buddhism, that trains people to live an abstemious lifestyle, that, in the end, fettered the enormous strength of the Mongols who in the Middle Ages had caused Asia and Europe to tremble.

Political Unrest

The geographical isolation of Mongolia, hemmed in as it is by Russia and China; its lack of mineral resources; and its lack of economic significance, formed for many years a natural protective barrier against the desire for conquest by the neighboring great powers. That changed in the first half of the 20th century. After the violent repression of the popular uprising of 1905 against Chinese foreign rule, led by the national hero, Ayush, the Mongolian Autonomists were able to liberate their country from Manchu rule in 1911 and – with the support of the Russian Tsarist Empire – to declare independence. Southern Mongolia also rose up, leading to a brief unification of the two Mongolian regions.

However, the Chinese army finally succeeded in suppressing the revolt in the south. Its subsequent attempt to occupy the north as well failed, however, because of the Russian troops. In the year 1915, the autonomy of northern Mongolia was finalized in a "Three Power Agreement" – between China, Russia, and Northern Mongolia. This led to the separation of "Outer" and "Inner" Mongolia, as we still know them today. The autonomous region, Nei Monggol Zizhiqu, or Inner Mongolia, was, however, not proclaimed until May 1947.

Nevertheless, in spite of the Three Power Agreement, "Outer Mongolia" did not calm down. Once again the neighboring countries thrust the land into a period of upheaval and political unrest. First, China occupied the country – and then the Russian White Guard, so that the waves of revolution in Mongolia's northern neighbor rolled ever deeper into the empire of the steppe.

Winning the struggle against the superior foreign powers was beyond the strength of the Mongol people (more than 100,000 men and boys were Lamaist monks; that represented one-sixth of the population of Mongolia at the time). Outer Mongolia thus fell temporarily into the hands of the counter-revolutionary Russian intruders. Not until 1920/1921 did the Mongol revolutionaries under Sühkbaatar and Choibalsan – assisted by the Soviets – succeed in overcoming the occupying troops of the Chinese and the White Guard.

Mongolia is a land of open spaces under skies that call for humility when you follow the inspiring formations in the clouds that mere imagination could not conceive (left-hand page). – When you spend a night camping at the mountain massif of the Tavan Bogd (above) or experience one of the fiery, glowing evening moods in the Gobi Desert (left), you feel that the expanse of space and sky is something that is no longer distant or strange.

Almost as soon as the Red Army had marched into the ancient temple city of Urga in 1921, the occupiers began with the restructuring of the Mongolian state system. Based on the Soviet pattern, they formed a communist government, the policies of which soon led to determined resistance on the part of the Lamaist monasteries and the Mongolian population. The climax was an uprising that was brutally repressed by the Soviet troops.

After this, Marshall Choibalsan (the "Stalin of Mongolia") subjected the country to thirty years of merciless "cleansing." Thousands of people, above all members of minority groups, were murdered. The atheism of the Stalinists did not stop short even at the Lamaist Buddhist monks, clad in their red or yellow robes. In addition, hundreds of monasteries and prayer houses were reduced to rubble.

See page 29

25

Historical Dates and Pictures

In the Stone Age, small groups of hunters and reindeer herders inhabit the region that corresponds to present-day Mongolia.

3rd century BC: The Asian Huns (Xiongnu) found the Empire of Hsiung-nu.

155 BC: The Huns are driven out of northern China; the Hunnic migration begins.

4th century AD: The Huns establish their empire at the Black Sea. 6th century: Turkic (Altaic) tribes advance into the region now known as Mongolia.

745: The Uyghur drive out the Old Turkish Turkic peoples and set up their own empire at the Orkhon River.

840: The Kyrgyz destroy the Uyghur Empire.

924: The Kitan Empire of the Tungus tribes expands into the heartland of Mongolia (Orkhon region).

1125: Collapse of the Kitan Empire.

11th century: Many nomadic clans unite to form small independent nations.

Around 1160: Temüjin, later known as Genghis Khan, is born.

1195: Temüjin unites all the Mongol tribes and becomes their supreme ruler.

1207–1224: Numerous Mongol campaigns of conquest in North China and Central Asia; Bukhara and Samarkand are destroyed.

1220: Genghis Khan founds Kharakhorum, the capital city of the Mongols.

1227: Genghis Khan dies after a campaign against the Western Xia (Tanguts).

1229: Ögödei (1186–1241), the third-oldest son of Genghis Khan, is elected as Khan.

1236–1240: Batu Khan, a grandson of Genghis Khan, conquers Russia; cities such as Moscow, Rostov and Kiev fall as they are stormed by the Mongols.

1241: The Mongols destroy the army of German-Polish knights at Liegnitz; Great Khan Ögödei dies.

1242: Batu Khan ends the campaign of conquest against Europe.

1260: At an imperial diet, Kublai proclaims himself "Great Khan" and founds the Yuan Dynasty (1271–1368), the name of which means approximately "earliest beginning;" he moves the Mongol capital from Kharakhorum to Beijing.

1333: The 13-year-old Togoontömör ascends the throne of the Great Khan.

1368: Togoontömör Khan is driven out by the Chinese; he flees with his court to Kharakhorum.

1388: Chinese Ming troops destroy Kharakhorum and occupy Mong.

1394: Death of Togoontömör Khan.

2

16th century: The rank of Great Khan loses authority and the Mongol tribes are fragmented.

1634: The Manchurians occupy the region of Inner Mongolia and subdue the Mongol principalities.

1644–1911: The Manchurian Qing Dynasty expands and extends to cover Mongolia, eastern Turkestan, Tibet, Burma (Myanmar) and Vietnam.

1911: The Qing Dynasty collapses; the last emperor abdicates. Numerous uprisings in Mongolia; separation of Outer Mongolia from China. Proclamation of autonomy under the rule of the spiritual leader of Mongol Lamaism: Bogd Khan.

1920: Troops of the White Guard march into Mongolia under the leadership of General Baron von Ungern-Sternberg. The Mongolian People's Party (MPP) is formed.

3

1921: Accompanied by Mongolian partisan groups (under Sükhbaatar), the Red Army destroys the White Russian Army at Kyakhta and marches into Urga. Formation of a provisional People's Revolutionary government. Bogd Khan remains in office as head of state until his death in 1924.

1924: Founding of the Mongolian People's Republic (MPR); first constitution.

1929–1938: Nationalization of private property and property of religious institutions. The communists castigate Lamaism; more than 700 monasteries and prayer houses are destroyed and thousands of monks murdered. The resistance of the Mongols to the collectivization of agriculture leads to violent uprisings.

1939: Soviet and Mongolian troops defeat the Japanese, who are trying to invade Mongolia, at the Battle of Khalkhyn Gol.

1941: The Soviets force the Mongolians to adopt their Cyrillic script.

1945: Mongolia declares war on Japan. Mongolia rejects Chinese supremacy and in a referendum votes for national independence. The People's Republic of China recognizes the independence of the MPR.

1961–1962: The Mongolian People's Republic (MPR) becomes a member of UNO and Comecon.

1974: Establishment of diplomatic relationships between Mongolia and the Federal Republic of Germany.

1987: Establishment of diplomatic relationships between Mongolia and the USA.

1989: The withdrawal of Soviet troops begins; an ever-growing opposition movement leads to numerous demonstrations for reform.

1990: Demonstrations and a hunger strike by 32 famous opposition politicians leads to the resignation of the communist Politburo of the Central Committee, the first free elections and the end of one-party domination by the MPRP.

1991: New democratic constitution. The name People's Republic is abolished; the new name of the country is Mongol Uls (Mongolia). Parliamentary elections confirm the MPRP as the governing party.

1993: Punsalmaagiin Ochirbat is elected as President in the first direct elections.

1996: The opposition party wins the parliamentary elections. Mendsaikhany Enkhsaikhan becomes Prime Minister.

1997: Natsagiin Bagabandi (MPRP) is elected as the new President.

1999: The third democratically elected government resigns; the fourth Prime Minister is Rinchinnyamyn Amarjargal.

2000: Thirteen parties stand for the parliamentary elections; the old MPRP wins 72 of the 76 seats. Lhamsurengiyn Enebish becomes Head of Government, and the new Prime Minister is Nambaryn Enkhbayar.

2002: Handing over of a ratification agreement to the UN for the Statute of the International Criminal Court at the Hague. In April, Tsakhiagiin Elbegdorj becomes Prime Minister.

2005: The former Prime Minister, Enkhbayar, becomes the third President of Mongolia; Elbegdorj remains Prime Minister.

January 2006: New coalition government under the leadership of the MPRP and with the participation of the Motherland Party and some smaller parties.

2006: American graduates' meeting: At the initiative of the Educational Advising and Resource Center and the US embassy, the "First National Conference of US Alumni in Mongolia" is held in Ulan Bator on 10.28.2006; topics include economic and social issues in Mongolia.

4

5

Not until nearly seventy years later did the Mongol population succeed in shaking off the imposed socialist decrees of the Soviets. Month-long hunger strikes and demonstrations led to the resignation of the Central Committee of the People's Revolutionary Party in May 1990 and to the abandoning of all dogma. The newly-won freedom took hold of a whole nation and people could revel in the joy of at last being able to be true Mongols once again.

Now the way was clear for elections in a multi-party system based on Western models. However, the memory of Genghis Khan and the desire for a resurrection of his mighty empire remained. Under the decades of rule by the Moscow-aligned Politburo, the name of Genghis Khan had been regarded in Mongolia as being reactionary – as it was in China too. The one-time ruler, seen as a

The religion that was borne by young and old lamas, survived in Mongolia even during the period of oppression by the state. Thus, splendidly-colored decorative pictures still adorn the Gandan Monastery in Ulan Bator, where pious Buddhists pray several times a day, take part in religious ceremonies, and read their holy books.

The Russian Explorer of Asia, Nikolai Przewalski

The last surviving species of wild horse was named after the Russian explorer of Asia, Nikolai Michailovich Przewalski (1839–1888), who discovered them in 1881 during one of his expeditions to Mongolia. At that time, Przewalski encountered a whole herd of this horse race, which now barely exists in the wild and can only be seen in zoos.

Nikolai Przewalski is regarded as the most important Russian explorer of Asia. On his first great journey through Asia – in the years 1870 to 1873 – he already covered 11,843 kilometers (7,402 miles) on horseback, visiting eastern Mongolia, northern Tibet and the area around Kuku Nor, before crossing the Gobi Desert from south to north and returning to Irkutsk via Urga.

His numerous journeys through Central Asia filled out large gaps in the knowledge of the time of areas on the map that were previously only blanks. He was awarded the Gold Medal of the London Geographical Society in 1879 for his achievements.

Przewalski's life dream was to explore Lhasa, the mysterious city in Tibet, the residence of the Dalai Lama. His dream was to remain unfulfilled; after drinking contaminated water in the magnificent landscape of Issyk-Kul, the huge mountain lake that now lies in Kyrgyzstan, he died on November 1, 1888 of typhus.

Ulan Bator: Around the outskirts of the city, many nomads who are looking for work have settled in yurts and simple houses (large photograph). – The central Sükhbaatar Square in Ulan Bator (top). – In the paleontology section of the Central Museum, there are impressive pictures and skeletons of carnivorous dinosaurs that have been excavated in the Gobi Desert (above). – Group photograph in front of the government building (bottom right).

"relic of feudalism," was not compatible with the aims of the communist system. All that changed with the disintegration of the Soviet Union and the fall of communism. Moreover, many Mongols regained their national identity through their reverence for Genghis Khan – an identity feared by some politicians in Mongolia, who strive to achieve more modernity and a free market economy.

The same politicians also fear the liberal thinking and lifestyle of the nomadic culture; many even consider these to be hopelessly backward, and would most like to abolish them. But the inhabitants of the Mongolian steppe, with their traditional way of life, are much too headstrong to sacrifice their world to modernity in the foreseeable future.

31

The Future Belongs to the Young People

The political and economic conditions in Mongolia – since the forced resignation of the Central Committee of the People's Revolutionary Party – can mainly be seen in the capital city, Ulan Bator (Ulaanbaatar), that lies at an altitude of 1350 meters in a wide valley, surrounded by the foothills of the Khentii Mountains.

South of the city, the "Holy Mountain," the Bogd Khan Uul massif (highest point: 2257 meters/ 7403 feet) towers in the distance. In front of it, gently rolling hills, almost treeless, reach into the city of 900,000 inhabitants.

Here, in the valley of the river Tuul Gol, Mongolian, Chinese, and Russian traders once established a caravan meeting point. In 1649 a monastery was founded at the same location as the headquarters of the Buddhist spiritual leader of Mongolia – and this was named "Urga." This name is derived from the word "orgo," meaning something like "palace of a most important person."

In 1924, the name "Urga" was changed to "Ulan Bator Khoto," meaning "city of the red heroes." The common usage is now Ulaanbaatar or Ulan Bator. In the largest city in Mongolia, you will now find small dwelling houses and innumerable uniform apartment blocks, built close together in the Soviet style, in which the majority of the people live in fairly basic conditions.

Concrete high-rise and tenement blocks, in front of which small horses, shaggy camels or heavily-loaded trucks can be seen, alternate with solid-fuel power stations and industrial plant, while on the outskirts the city is surrounded by a ring of yurts. Places of interest are the Gandan Monastery, founded in 1838, a center of Sutra-Tantra Buddhism, and the temple complex of Bogdo Khan, also known as the Palace Museum – a fascinating complex that was built between 1893 and 1912 as the winter residence of the last spiritual leader of Mongolia.

Moreover, Ulan Bator is the commercial, cultural and, above all, political center of the Mongol people. In July 1992, the "Mongolian People's Revolutionary Party" (the communist party that wielded sole power from 1924 to 1990) won a landslide victory here in the second free parliamentary elections.

Nevertheless, the future of Mongolia belongs to the young people; 70 percent of the population is less than 30 years of age. This generation of young people wishes to make their country the "Switzerland of the East," with computers and western-style dress. This is no easy undertaking, for outside the cities, the Mongols still live as a people on horseback in a land with more horses than people. The old Mongol script is back on the school curriculum; there there is religious freedom once more; and the people stream to the few Lama temples that were not destroyed by the Stalinists.

In addition, the search for a new identity will continue to be overshadowed by the past for a long time: above all by the power and greatness of Genghis Khan, who once gave his people the honorary title "Mongol" – meaning "the courageous ones."

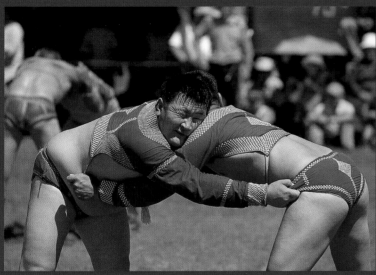

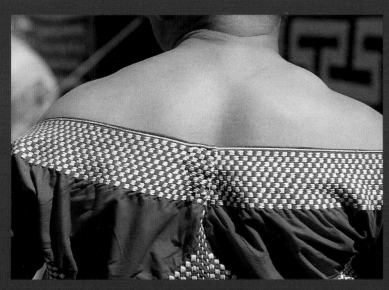

The Mongols still love to ride horses, especially at the annual Nadaam. The tradition of this festival goes back to even before the time of Genghis Khan. In those days the "Golden Horde" marched to Hungary and Silesia; today the young jockeys, mostly girls and boys aged between five and 13 years wearing colorful riding caps, compete in races across the grasslands.

Fall landscape in the Gobi Altai.

Report from Beijing

Kublai Khan and Marco Polo

1 Mongol campaign of conquest in China under Kublai Khan around the year 1275; Indian miniature, about 1590.

2 The four chief wives of Kublai Khan with their children (book illustration from the year 1375).

3 The brothers Nicola and Maffeo Polo being welcomed by Kublai Khan on their first journey to Asia (book illustration, about 1412).

"A million lies" is what they called the reports of the world traveler, Marco Polo (1254 to 1324) in his native city of Venice, on his return from China, when he told stories of the lifestyle at the court of the Mongol Great Khan, Kublai, where once the courtly splendor had no equal in the world.

The early feudal Mongol Empire experienced its flowering under the leadership of Kublai Khan (a grandson of the founder of the Mongol Empire, Genghis Khan) who became Great Khan in 1259 and was closely oriented to the Chinese culture. It was also Kublai who moved the seat of the Mongol rulers – from Kharakhorum in the steppe of his native land to conquered Beijing. There, the outer walls of his center of power enclosed an area of 64 square kilometers (25 square miles). Each fortress wall was eight kilometers (5 miles) in length and the inner walls measured six kilometers (3.8 miles). In the center was the palace, one kilometer in length and the same in width, which was filled with priceless treasures. The clothes of the emperor alone filled two buildings, and in his stables there were ten thousand white stallions.

Kublai Khan, who founded the Mongol Yuan Dynasty (1271–1368), also created the largest coherent state that had ever existed in Asia at that time. But the excessive striving for power by individual princes and the mentality of Kublai Khan, who became more and more Chinese, finally heralded the beginning of the decline of the empire. Even before the fall of the Mongol Empire, the Venetian Marco Polo had arrived at the court of Kublai Khan in the year 1271. Barely thirty years earlier, Europe had trembled before the cavalry of the Mongols. The three members of the Polo family – Marco, his father Nicola, and his uncle Maffeo – had first visited the Holy Land before traveling through Persia, Afghanistan, the Pamir Mountains and the Takla-

2

makan Desert, using the southern Silk Road to finally reach Beijing.

In 1275, they stood in the presence of Kublai Khan. Marco, who was 21 years old at the time, remained for 17 years in the service of the Khan and undertook many journeys through China and Southeast Asia as an envoy of the Khan. During this time, Marco Polo gained much insight into the Mongol state within China, bringing back detailed reports of this when he returned to Venice.

He told of social institutions and splendid military highways, of canals that linked rivers together; he praised the public hospitals in which those who were ill or injured were cared for, extolled the feeding of the poor, from which about 20,000 of the poorest people in Peking benefited; and the many warehouses from which people could buy food cheaply in times of famine.

Furthermore, Marco Polo learnt

about paper money, made from the inner bark of the mulberry tree, and used as a means of payment. But the most surprising thing for the Venetians was the freedom of religion in the multiracial state of Kublai Khan. Whether Christian, Buddhist, Moslem or shamanist, everyone was permitted to worship his god or his idols publicly. Marco Polo

3

tells about Kublai Khan himself in detail in his book "Il Milione", usually known as "The Travels of Marco Polo" or the "Description of the World."

"Kublai Khan is the sixth Great Khan, that is, the sixth ruler over all Tatars. (…) Because of his boldness and industry, because of his wisdom, he has been given power. (…) Since the beginning of

his rule until the present year forty two years have passed; Kublai Khan is now possibly about eighty five years of age. (…) The most powerful ruler of all rulers, known by the name of Kublai Khan, is a noble character. He is neither too tall nor too small, but of medium stature. He is a strong man with well-formed limbs. His face is rosy-white; his eyes dark and glowing and his nose has a fine profile.

He has four wives and calls each of them his chief wife; (…) the four wives have borne the Khan twenty two sons. The oldest was called Genghis out of love for the good Genghis Khan; he was destined to later become Great Khan of the entire empire. He died prematurely and yet he left a son called Temur. This Temur is designated to be the future Great Khan, and this is for one single reason: because he is the son of the firstborn of the great Khan."

In the Realm of the Taiga

From North to West to East

In the north of Mongolia, where taiga landscapes, mountain massifs and huge lakes shape the world of nature, the unspoiled quality and endlessness of the land are ever-present. The land is complemented by the sky as an impressive ally; scenery is revealed that could be described as "exalted"; and

Horses are the most beloved companions of the Mongols. There are still more horses in Mongolia than people (above and right). – More than 500 stelae with engravings of deer can be seen today in the wild steppe. These "deer stones" from the Bronze Age or Iron Age mark burial places of people of high rank (right-hand page).

the wide expanses seem exhilarating, even though many corners of it are rocky and almost inaccessible. Here, north of Ulan Bator (Ulaanbaatar), we find the highland area of the Khentii, the lowest mountain range in Mongolia.

With peaks rising to heights of up to 2,800 meters (8,960 feet), these mountains do not have either eternal snow or glaciers, although the traces of a former ice sheet are particularly apparent in the central section of the Khentii. Besides the U-shaped valleys, moraines and glacial lakes that characterize the region, three large rivers of Mongolia also rise here: the Kherlen (1,250 kilometers/ 781 miles in length) the Onon (808 km/ 505 miles) and the Tuul (704 km/ 488 miles).

Thanks to these rivers, the watercourses in the Khentii carry water permanently, forming a fairly dense network. In this respect, the Khentii Mountains far exceed all other regions of Mongolia. Moreover, the Mongolian Khentii forms the eastern flank of a massive curved range of mountains, at the center of

RUSSIA / MONGOLIA / CHINA (inset map)

R U S S I A

In Mongolia, not only men are seen in a saddle; women also drive the yak herds across the grass steppe to the camp (center). Chopping wood for a camp fire in the taiga (below).

which rises the Khangai Massif. The main range of the Khentii is extremely rugged. From the center, foothills reach out in all directions. While the steep western slopes, deeply dissected by gorges, are permeated by swampy valleys and scattered boulders, the southern slopes fall relatively gently. Wide, dry valleys have formed between the gentle hills that give way to long ridges of undulating land in the east.

In the north, by contrast, the scenery is typical of the mountain taiga: birch forests and moors grow above the permafrost layer, and the tall and slender Siberian stone pine (Pinus sibiricus) covers entire slopes and mountains. Other varieties of tree are the Siberian larch (Larix sibirica), the Siberian spruce (Picea obovata), the Scots pine (Pinus silvestris) and the Siberian fir (Abies sibirica). Also typical of the highland taiga are cranberries (Vaccinium vitis idaea), which sometimes form a thick carpet in the pine forests. Other vegetation includes green alder, mountain willow, rhododendrons, and bilberries, which

can be found growing on the forest floor in many regions. As the taiga is often completely empty and uninhabited, many animals live here, including the Siberian elk, wild boar, elk, pica (whistling hare), squirrel, chipmunk and flying squirrel. More rare are the brown bear, marten, ermine, weasel, and sable.

42

RUSSIA

CHINA

Kyachta
chig Sukhbaatar
Schaamar
Khuder
Darkhan
Bugant
SELENGE
Scharyngol
Baruunkharaa

Verkhniy
Ul'Khun
Bayandun
Bayan Uul
Dadal

MONGOL DARIGANGA
NATURE RESERVE
Ereenzav
UGTAM
NATURE RESERVE
Wall of Genghis Kahn

Bayantal
Khalkhgol
Buir
Nuur
Sumber
Yirxie

HAN HENTEYN
NATURE RESERVE
Batschireet
Binder
Bayan
Adraga
Norovlin

Tschoybalsan

NUMRUG
NATURE RESERVE

Zhargalant
Batsumber
khontuul
Bayantschandmani
GORKHI TERELDSH
NATURE RESERVE
Ulan Bator
Baganuur
KHUSTAJN UUL
NATURE RESERVE
Lun
Nalaykh
Bayan
Erdenesant
CENTRAL AIMAQ
Bayanmunk

KHENTII
Berkh
Batnorov
Bayan
Ovoo
SUKHBAATAR
Undurkhaan
Munkkhaan
Baruun Urt

Kherlen Gol
DORNOD
EASTERN MONGOLIA
NATURE RESERVE
Matad

Orchon Gol
ge Murun
Orkhon
Tuul Gol

At higher altitudes, the mountain taiga is overshadowed by flattened peaks protruding from the dense belt of forest. Usually these are flat, almost table-like hilltops of bare rock that are covered with boulders and periglacial scree. These flattened, bare mountain-tops are known as golzy which means something like "bald head."

Towards the south, the forests of the taiga become less and less dense; the Mongolian steppe begins to take over. The farthest fringes of the Khentii taiga forests lie approximately 70 kilometers (44 miles) southeast of Ulan Bator. Here in the southern Khentii Mountains, with their large population of wild animals, individual mountain groups tower up, the most important of which is Tsetsee Gun Peak (2,257 meters/ 7,403 feet). It is part of the Bogd Khan Uul massif and one of the Mongolians' favorite mountains, revered since times long past. Its picturesque slopes are celebrated in song, as are the peaceful lakes and remote valleys. The transition from the mixed forest zone to Siberian larch forest, the so-called mountain taiga, is particularly striking here.

Above the tree line, the untouched tundra – lichens and moss – forms the summit regions before expanses of granite massifs with huge boulders. A bizarre sight on the southwest flank of the Khentii is a labyrinth of small sandstone outcrops, shaped by wind erosion, which resemble yurts when seen from a distance.

In 1678, the region around the Bogd Uul was designated a nature protection area by Zanabazar, the highest dignitary of Buddhism. Since those days, it has been considered one of the oldest of its kind in the world. Even before the expansion of Buddhism in Mongolia, there were numerous places of religious pilgrimage. Today, many legends persist about the mountain.

Many grandfathers take pleasure in looking after their grandchildren.

Magical effects of light at a lake in northern Mongolia.

43

Genghis Khan's Birthplace

In northern Mongolia, near the Russian border, lies the town of Tsagaan Nuur. Here, by the lake of the same name, local people are building a hut using the most basic tools. When the walls have been erected, moss will be pushed between the tree trunks as insulation.

This area in the Khentii Mountains, to the northeast of Ulan Bator, is also the location of the supposed birthplace of Genghis Khan. This is suggested by several statements in "The Secret History of the Mongols." Buddhist prayer flags still flatter in the wind at Deluun Boldog, a 1,231-meter (4,038-foot) mountain near the center of the Binder sum, which experts believe to have been the birthplace. Sacrificial offerings lie on a memorial stone that bears the inscription, "Deluun Boldog – Genghis Khan – in the year of the water horse – born in the year 1162, on May 16, at full moon."

Unfortunately, the "Secret History" does not tell us anything about Genghis Khan's burial or burial place. And so for decades, archeologists and adventurers have been searching for the last resting place of the world ruler, who is still regarded as a guardian by many Mongols.

44

Where Working and Living are Inseparable

Remote and mysterious lies the lake of Khuvsgul Nuur in the far north of Mongolia. It is a huge lake – 134 kilometers (84 miles) long, 39 kilometers (24 miles) wide and 262 meters (859 feet) deep – and is also known as the "blue pearl of Mongolia" because of its intense color. Surrounded by barely accessible mountains and dense forests, Lake Khuvsgul is an inland sea with rich stocks of fish where thousands of seagulls and cormorants circle. Not without reason is this region known as the "Switzerland of Mongolia."

From all sides, the alpine Khuvsgul Mountains stretch down to the lake. Mountainous peninsulas alternate with small headlands and river estuaries. Then, wide valleys open up again, with swampy banks, wide sandbanks or tranquil lagoons. Bears and wolves prowl in the higher and more isolated regions.

But nomads also live here: the Darkhad people, of whom only a few dozen still live in the northernmost regions of Mongolia, as well as the Tsaatan, a small group of nomadic reindeer herders who, like the Darkhad, are one of around thirty minority groups in Mongolia.

Like their ancestors, the Tsaatan live in round tents. They are in danger of dying out, because their tribe now numbers barely 40 families. They roam through the land with their herds of reindeer – a land that, like their lifestyle, is reduced to the basic elements. This does not mean poverty or need, but creates space for what is essential, so that for the Tsaatan there is no division between life and work.

This is reflected in their faces that are weathered by sun, wind and cold. Their most striking feature is their eyes: accustomed to wide open spaces and seemingly unfathomable, they seem to be from another planet.

45

In the steppe and desert, water is absolutely vital; sometimes the nomads carry the precious liquid in buckets to their camp from rivers or wells (below). After milking, something the Mongols are very skilled at, the milk is poured into a centrifuge to separate the cream. Then, butter is made by hand, while the delicious cheese is cut with a thread (right-hand page).

Some years ago, the only steamship of the Mongolian merchant navy still sailed across Lake Khuvsgul – from Khatgal, previously an important port at the southern end of the vast lake, to Khankh (also called Turta) at the northern tip, not far from the Russian border. But when economic conditions in the former Soviet Union became precarious, the ferry service between the south and the north end of the lake was stopped. Now, the ferry lies at anchor, and Khatgal is declining into a ghost town.

Furthermore, the enormous surface of water of Lake Khuvsgul, which has many similarities with Lake Baikal in Russia, strongly influences the climate of the surrounding region – causing thick clouds, heavy showers and the coolest summer of any part of Mongolia.

It is never really calm here. The winds snarl almost unceasingly across the landscape. Even in June there is a likelihood of frost and snow, while in winter temperatures can fall to below

50° Celsius. It is easy to understand why many Mongols refer to this part of their country as the "end of the world."

The Coldest Region of Mongolia

To the west and southwest, the foothills of the Khangai Mountains are hemmed in by the Khan Khukhii mountain range, that rises steeply from the "Great Lakes Basin." In this natural basin, there are huge salt lakes with no outlet, for example Ogiy Nuur, Orog Nuur, Khjargas Nuur and Khar Us Nuur.

In the northernmost basin of this region lies the salt lake, Uvs Nuur. With an area of 3,350 square kilometers (1,293 square miles), this is the largest lake in Mongolia. It is fed mainly by the river Ongin, although the river's floodwaters do not always reach the lake; now and again the waters seep away into the sand, and then the lake dries out and becomes a regular salt pan.

Because of the high salt content of the water, the Uvs Nuur is not useful for any commercial enterprise. There are no fish in the lake. Only migrating birds use this region for nesting. In the winter, Uvs Nuur is one of the coldest places of Mongolia. Then, temperatures as low as 57° Celsius have been recorded.

The East – Volcanoes, Swamps, Wide Steppes

Eastern Mongolia, where the Siberian taiga meets the Mongolian steppe, is dominated by extensive peneplains with gently undulating and hilly landscapes. Stretching for hundreds of kilometers, the plains do not vary much. Wide depressions and flat basins with salt marshes and long earthen rises are the dominant features. This monotonous scenery is interrupted occasionally by single granite outcrops or basalt volcanic cones.

The heart of the southeast is the Khalkh Plain with the East Mongolian Depression, which lies at a height of less than 1,000 meters (3,280 feet) and is up to 100 kilometers (63 miles) in width. Large areas of salt marsh and small, shallow salt lakes characterize the landscape; the western section is almost entirely devoid of flowing watercourses. On the other hand, the Kherlen River maintains adequate water levels as its floodwaters flow through the eastern regions of this dry steppe landscape. Along the banks, the lush green meadows and pastureland form a sharp contrast to the gray-green shades of the feather grass steppe.

To the south, a basalt volcanic landscape adjoins the Eastern Mongolian Depression; here, you will find lapilli and kilometer-

See page 50

Fishing in a Primeval Landscape

Lake Khuvsgul

1 Evening mood on the eastern shore of Lake Khuvsgul.

2 All hands are needed to manage the many meters of fishing net, when the fishermen land their catch.

At the point where the eastern Siberian taiga meets with Mongolian territory lie the densely-forested Khuvsgul Mountains. Towards the north lie the foothills of the Eastern Sayan Mountains; in the southeast extend the ridges of the Tannu-Ola Mountains, which also form part of the range. Here, at the Russian-Mongolian border, is also the Munku-Sardyk massif with its fields of firn and hanging glaciers, and with peaks rising to a height of 3,491 meters (11, 450 feet).

In the midst of this high mountain massif with its strong alpine contours, lies a magical lake: Khuvsgul Nuur. Surrounded by gigantic rugged peaks and larch forests, it is like a giant inland sea lying at an altitude of 1,624 meters (5,327 feet). With a surface area of 2,620 square kilometers (1,011 square miles), it is the second-largest lake in Mongolia and, with a depth of 262 meters (859 feet), the deepest in Central Asia. During the winter months it freezes over completely. Then the ice occasionally reaches a thickness of one-and-a-half meters (5 feet), so that trucks can even transport goods across its 134-kilometer (84-mile) length and 39-kilometer (24-mile) width.

In order to preserve the character of this unique natural landscape, and to prevent the extinction of the wealth of flora and fauna, Lake Khuvsgul and the surrounding shores have been designated a national park. Here, more than 240 species of birds can be found, including whooper swans, mute swans and a huge variety of species of ducks and seagulls.

Furthermore, this freshwater lake, like almost all lakes and rivers in Mongolia, is rich in fish: trout and carp, pike, sturgeon, catfish and the common perch are among the some 70 species found here.

In the 1950s, a Russian placed spawn from the Baikal omul fish (Coregonus autumnalis), which is indigenous to Lake Baikal, in Lake Khuvsgul. It is a tasty fish that grows to two kilograms in weight. In addition, the first industrial spawning plant was started at Lake Khuvsgul, so that freshwater fishing here currently has the most successful quota in the country. Up to 3,000 decitons per annum are caught.

3–7 *The second-largest lake in Mongolia has an idyllic, purely natural setting; here there are dense forests and beautiful meadows with daisies and edelweiss – not forgetting the stony shores and lonely bays where the children of the local people sit in front of their little huts. – 8 On the way back to Khatgal, a town at the southern tip of Lake Khuvsgul.*

4

Not only is the northernmost lake in Mongolia one of the most beautiful, but it is also one of the clearest in the world.

In bright sunlight, one can see to a depth of twenty meters into the water. Scientists have discovered rare hydroflora and hitherto unknown benthos and plankton organisms during hydrobiological research.

Nevertheless, the Mongolian environmentalists in this region still face many challenges, especially since the discovery of large resources of rock phosphate in the vicinity of Lake Khuvsgul. Mining of these underground beds would without any doubt destroy the ecological balance of the lake.

5

6

7

8

49

wide lava flows between fertile grasslands and herbal steppe. Weathered volcanic cones and rugged basalt cliffs tower up, as a reminder of the Quaternary period when the earth here was in violent turmoil.

Almost 200 volcanoes, many of which were still active only a few thousand years ago, and innumerable lava caves, that are probably among the most impressive in Mongolia, typify the landscape of Dariganga in the southeast of the country. Many of the scattered volcanoes have retained their conical shape until the present day, while others have collapsed like ruins. Shiliin Bogd Uul (1,778 m/ 5,832 feet) is the highest point of volcanic origin and rises more than 400 meters (1,312 feet) above a gently rolling grass steppe. From the edge of the crater there are expansive views into China.

Not less significant is Altan Ovoo (1,354 m/ 4,441 feet), also called Dari Ovoo. At intervals of three years (1997, 2000, 2003, etc.) the second-largest festival of the Mongolians is celebrated

at the foot of the mountain. It is similar to the famous Nadaam Festival and also features the traditional Mongolian sports – wrestling, archery and riding.

Altan Ovoo, the "Golden Mountain," has also been revered by the Dariganga people as a holy mountain since earliest times. They are a centuries-old nomadic people which speaks its own dialect and which is related to neighboring tribes in Inner Mongolia. According to the beliefs of the Dariganga, no woman is permitted to climb Altan Ovoo.

High up on the peak of Altan Ovoo once stood a legendary Buddhist temple with a golden roof that reached up into the clouds. Three hundred lamas are said to have lived here on the mountain and were provided with food – millet, flour and tea – by the Dariganga nomads.

Now the temple buildings are in ruins, and the lamas have moved to other regions. Only three stone figures of human forms that were carved in granite in the 12th century in honor of a king,

In northern Mongolia: mountain peaks glow in evening light near Ulaan Uul. – At the foot of high mountains, Mongolian horses traverse almost impassable terrain (below).

Wedding Rituals

The Mongolian language does not have a specific term for the word "wedding." The usual expression is *khurim*, meaning something like "banquet." Another common usage is *sine ger barikh*, "erecting a new yurt;" this also explains the ritual of constructing the yurt during a wedding party.

But first there is the ritual of wooing the bride, in which a marriage broker is commissioned to respectfully request consent to the wedding at the house of the chosen one. If the parents of the bride accept the offer, a meal is arranged in honor of the suitor. In some regions, it was once the custom to have a lama, who was also an astrologer, read the horoscope, to find out if the couple were suited to each other. Today, a bride price is still negotiated, and this may range from one sheep to whole herds, according to the wealth of the family.

The formal wedding feast, that always lasts for several days, is called *nair*. It is a very disciplined affair in which singers and official speakers proclaim blessings on the couple and their new yurt, and these contributions are among the finest that Mongolian folklore has produced.

a queen and a prince still stand at the foot of the southeastern slopes. These stelae are still revered by believers who place their sacrificial offerings here.

Similar figures, under which the dead were once buried, can also still be found in the region of the Moltsog Sand Dunes (Dariganga sum). Chiseled out of granite or volcanic tuff, many of these statues were damaged during the early periods of tribal feuding by enemies of the deceased persons. Even during the dark chapters of the more recent past, when the repression by the communist regime reached into the farthest corners of Mongolia, the heads of many of these statues were severed. Many of the stone heads have in the meantime been recovered and have been restored to their original location.

Farther to the east, the land is shaped by the Eastern Mongolian Plateau, the farthest extremity of which resembles a finger. Situated approximately in the center, this steppe-like high plateau is interrupted by a wide depression: an oversized, flat basin with furrowed, undulating plains and fields of rock and pebble scree. Between the salt pans and sand fields there are salt lakes and marshes with only a little steppe flora.

Here and there, you will come across low saxaul trees with their gnarled trunks and branches formed into bizarre sculptures over the centuries. In this region, you cannot fail to notice that the wind gradually gains the upper hand, especially during the extreme drought of summer.

To the south and east of the plain, the dissected terrain rises again to the foothills of the "Great Khingan" that stretch from north to south. The national border between China and Mongolia runs across the highest point of this mountain range.

A Mongolian girl wearing her best outfit at Tsagaan Nuur (above). Areas of dense forest cover northern Mongolia. A paradise for flora and fauna.

52

Reindeer carry the possessions of the Tsaatan to their next camp.

Reindeer Herders at the End of the World:

The Last Freedom of the Tsaatan

1 Without any cares, a small Tsaatan child lies snugly wrapped in a blanket.
2 Selling reindeer antlers.
3 In the morning light, a reindeer strolls to drink at a river in the Khuvsgul Mountains.
4 After firmly lashing the saddle, baggage is loaded onto a reindeer.
5 In the wilds of nature, the Tsaatan set up their mobile tents.
6 Following their traditional pastoral circuits, the Tsaatan migrate along the ancient routes through northern Mongolia.

In the far north of Mongolia, in the regions of the Khuvsgul Mountains and the huge inland sea of Lake Khuvsgul, the last herds of wild reindeer in Mongolia can be found. These animals are smaller than red deer and have branched antlers covered in velvet-like fur. They are now very few in number. Therefore, they have been placed under state protection.

The last families of the Mongolian tribe of the Tsaatan live in this remote region, to the northwest of Lake Khuvsgul, and far from any large city. They make a living from their domesticated reindeer herds. The reindeer nomads, who

call themselves *Tuvin* or *Tuva*, are members of the Soyon Uriankhai people group. They are a people that is threatened with extinction, as they number barely more than thirty or forty families. Untouched nature and a magnificent landscape with inaccessible, 3,000-meter-high mountains (10,000 feet) and one of the sources of the Yenisei River, the fifth-longest river of Russia, form the backdrop for their home.

The Tsaatan still live, as their ancestors did, in simple, circular tents that consist of birch stems, loosely bound together, on which large reindeer skins or tarpaulins

56

6

are fixed. They transport their mobile dwellings by camels, following their instincts to roam in a fixed yearly cycle as they adapt to the pastoral habits of their reindeer herds. These animals, whose falling and rising antlers seem to move through the landscape with the regular rolling motion of a wave, determine the bare existence of the Tsaatan, who have always hunted animals for their fur and bred reindeer, as the Laplanders also do.

From generation to generation, the Tsaatan have handed down the route for their migrations from the pasturelands near Lake Khuvsgul to the taiga at the Russian border. This knowledge and their adaptability to a harsh and extreme environment form the basis for their existence. The Tsaatan in northern Mongolia thus still have a close affinity with primeval nature. Here, in this uninhabited region that seems like an oversized patchwork of mountains, rivers, swamps and taiga, the wilderness also fosters isolation. Thus, the tribe of the Tsaatan has always been divided into family clans. Their Turkic language provided the only common link between the Tuvin tribes, who also live in the Chinese province of Sinkiang and in the Russian taiga.

The daily struggle against a hostile environment was, and is, the purpose in life of the Tsaatan, whose language, script, religion, songs and legends have scarcely been recorded. Their reindeer live on leaves, stems, grasses, buds and bushes. This fodder, rich in proteins and minerals, compensates for the one-sided and poor nourishment from mosses and lichens during the winter months. Naturally, the reindeer must bring a yield for the Tsaatan within the cycle of their year-round pastoral economy. It supplies not only meat, but in the lactation period, also thirty to forty liters of milk, with a fat content of around seven percent. The skin is used to make boots and winter clothing and to cover the yurts. Also, the Tsaatan use the reindeer for riding and as a pack animal, as it can carry loads of up to 70 kilograms.

A visit to the Tsaatan requires several weeks and much effort. Offroad vehicles can travel in summer only as far as the administrative district (sum) of Tsagaan Nuur.

Those who wish to travel farther, without having to use a helicopter, must cover a distance of 80 to 100 kilometers (50 to 63 miles) riding horses or reindeer. There, in a largely untouched natural environment, where loneliness prevails and silence is everpresent, the traveler may discover that this lifestyle of the Tsaatan that is doomed is, in itself, a challenge to preserve a way of life that is often thoughtlessly destroyed in the name of the progress that is termed "civilization."

57

Volcanoes, Lakes and High Peaks

The Khangai Mountains – in the Heart of Mongolia

"The Mongols handed us three robes with the words, 'You will not take gold and silver, but you have spent a long time here, praying for the Khan. He therefore requests that each of you at least accept this simple robe, so that you do not go away from him empty-handed.' Then we had no other choice but to accept them for awe of him, for they are very offended when their gifts are rejected."
Wilhelm von Rubruk, *Journey to the Court of the Great Khan Mongke*

A Mongol at Terkhin Tsagaan Lake travels with his yak cart through the Khangai Mountains (above). Mongol girl wearing the traditional deel (right). – At the Orkhon waterfall. From a height of about 20 meters (66 feet), the waters of the Ulaan River plunge into the Orkhon (right-hand page).

The contrasts could not be greater: magnificent mountain massifs, bizarre volcanoes, wide valleys, green meadows, foaming rivers and picturesque lakes that glitter like mirrors in the clear sunlight. And high above, strange cloud shapes being driven along in the blue sky by the whistling wind. All this is to be found in the heartlands of Mongolia, in the center of the country.

The traveler will discover here breathtaking scenery in a pristine state, that sometimes gives rise to the spine-chilling feeling of being completely alone on the planet. You will experience all the enchantment of Mongolia: remote corners and bare rocky realms, in which human life is virtually unknown and which, nonetheless, also form the backbone of the Mongol Empire.

Mongolia is, generally speaking, a typical highland region. Eighty-five percent of the land lies above 1,000 meters (3,280 feet). The central mountains of the Khangai, consisting mainly of granite and crystalline rocks, rise even higher. Now and again – especially in the eastern Khangai – you will come across black-

brown lava sheets with large fields of boulders, cracked cliffs and volcanic cones.

The main ridge of the imposing Khangai Mountains rises from 2,600 meters (8,528 feet) in the east to a height of 3,400 meters (11,152 feet) in the west. Seemingly endless high plains displaying evidence of plateau glaciation from the Pleistocene period extend over large areas, above which tower the solitary alpine massifs. Small hanging glaciers fall steeply into the valleys that have been carved deep into the mountains. Rivers in full spate have carved out deep gorges with equal power, so that in the Khangai Mountains a vast network of streams and rivers has developed. They flow from all directions to join the Selenge, of which the Orkhon is the largest tributary.

The Selenge is the river that carries most water in Mongolia. Its speed of flow varies frequently during its long journey over 992 kilometers (620 miles) to Lake Baikal – 593 kilometers (370 miles) of them through Mongolian territory. In comparison, the Orkhon, a mountain river with an abundance of fish, that rises on the Suvarga Khairkhan mountain (3,200 meters/ 10,496 feet), attains a length of around 1,120 kilometers (700 miles).

Starting as a small mountain stream, it grows to a raging torrent as it flows northwards, and its wild waters have carved bizarre gorges out of the rocks. With a steep gradient and varying widths, it races over numerous cliffs and boulders before it gradually calms down and then winds in large meanders through a gentle landscape that Mongolians like to celebrate in song. Here, beside the Orkhon river, in a wide and scenic valley, lies the most significant historical site of Mongolia: Kharakhorum. Now, only ruins of the legendary capital city founded by Genghis Khan remain, and these are not particularly inspiring. But looking back on its history, it is easy to imagine what the city must once have looked like, when the Mongol rulers were writing world history.

Free-roaming Przewalski horses that were released southwest of Ulan Bator (top). Khangai Mountains: At the mountain lake Terkhin Tsagaan Nuur (2060 m), yak herds carry their loads through open country. – School-girls near Uliastai.

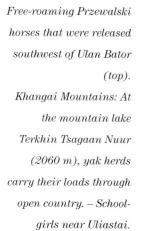

At that time, in the early 13th century, the location of Kharakhorum – as the political and cultural capital of the Mongols – was well chosen. The wide, sweeping Orkhon valley, lying at an altitude of 1,500 meters (4,920 feet), was the ideal location for a settlement of several thousand people who needed to find

food for their everyday sustenance. Furthermore, the waters of the Orkhon were even then diverted for irrigation, while huge tracts of grazing land were available for the cattle and herds of horses, and all the wood that was required was cut in the forests of the nearby Khangai Mountains.

Now, 500 years after Chinese troops razed Kharakhorum in the year 1388, German and Mongolian researchers are attempting to excavate the former capital of the Mongols. This is a difficult undertaking, as the founding of the city by nomads is a still considered a unique event.

Nevertheless, scientists have been able to reconstruct a model of Kharakhorum as it looked in the year 1254 – using aerial photographs, digital profiles of the earth and extensive excavations. The template the researchers used was the travel account by the Flemish Franciscan monk, William of Rubruck who traveled to Mongolia in the years 1253 to 1255 as an envoy of the French king, Louis IX (Saint Louis) – and who actually reached the court of the Great Khan in Kharakhorum.

Places Where the Presence of Invisible Powers can be Felt

Traversing the magnificent landscapes in the Khangai highlands, the traveler is repeatedly overcome by a feeling of being totally superfluous, even out of place. The influence of air, water and earth sometimes seem overpowering. Everything appears so full of light and so free. And when one encounters a family of nomads, livestock herders or arable farmers, one can read in

61

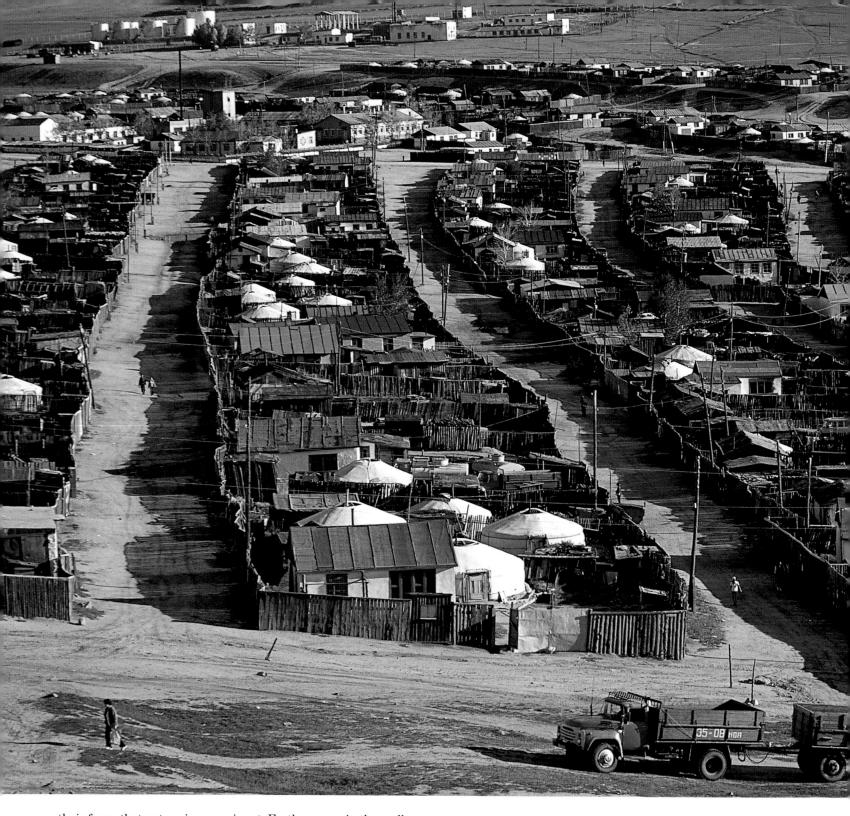

their faces that nature is preeminent. Furthermore, in the endless expanse of this huge landscape of mountains, valleys and rivers, one is constantly aware of the presence of higher, invisible powers. Perhaps these are gods, demons or spirits who watch over the lonely watercourses, deep gorges and high passes.

Each peak is a throne. And on each peak resides a powerful god. That could be true of the northern slope of the main ridge of the Khangai, with the mighty peaks of Tarabagatai. The highest points are Sodvon Uul (3,238 m/ 10,620 ft) and Dsagastuin Ula (3,161 m/ 10,368 ft). The mountain range descends gently towards the north, where many rivers flow, joining the Ider river in the

62

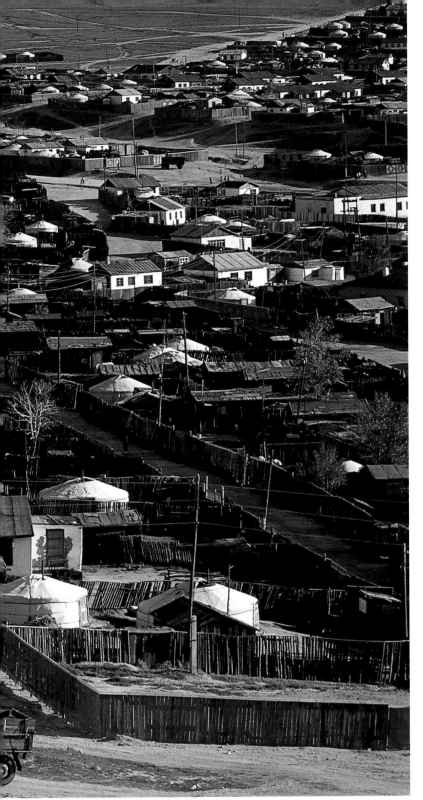

The Secret of the *Urga* –
The Mongolian Shepherd's Rod

To catch animals that have run away, the Mongols use a long shepherd's rod with a loop that functions rather like a lasso. The rod, known as an *urga*, is a relic from a time long past, when there was less civilization, but more culture.

Since ancient times, the *urga* has had not only a technical or warlike aspect. Adorned with a fiery-red colored cloth, it also has a romantic attribute: because the yurt, the dwelling tent, is not particularly conducive to the arousal of the senses, since everyone (man, wife, grandmother, grandfather and the children) sleeps under the same roof, the Mongol and his beloved have to turn to the steppe, where there is virtually no hiding place. When a Mongol man and a Mongol woman wish to be left alone, they simply ram the long shepherd's rod into the earth – a sign that no one should disturb them. No Mongol would dare to approach a place where a fiery-red colored cloth, attached to a shepherd's rod, is fluttering in the wind.

midst of a wide, forested steppe landscape. Here, larch forests and steppe valleys alternate with damp meadows and marshes.

The labyrinthine, rugged curve of the Khangai mountains stretches for more than 700 kilometers (438 miles) diagonally across Mongolia, from the Tsetsen Khairkhan in the west to the Deger Khan in the east. The highest peak of this striking mountain range is called *Otgon Tenger* ("youngest son of the heaven") and rises to a height of 4,021 meters (13,188 feet). Its white cap of snow and firn ice can be recognized from great distances across the land. Between the northern foothills of the Khangai Mountains and the Bolnai Massif, there is a high plateau with

lakes of impressive beauty. Like strings of beads, hundreds of mostly small lakes form a remote lake district. These lakes, presumably part of a huge network of watercourses that once had an outlet beyond the Khangai Mountains, are nearly all salt lakes.

The only really large freshwater lake in the region of the Khangai Mountains is the lake Ogiy Nuur, with an area of 25 square kilometers (9.6 square miles). Lying at an altitude of 1,337 meters (4,385 feet), it is fed from the south by the river Chuchschin Orkhon. Every year about 80 tonnes of fish are caught in its waters: pike, catfish and various kinds of perch. The region around Lake Ogiy is also home to numerous species of birds.

Magical-mystical atmosphere at a lake near Hoogen Haan (below). – Khangai Mountains: in the valley of the Ider river, the landscape seems like a primeval image of an ideal world (bottom). – In the light of the evening sun, a yak herd is driven to the camp of the herders. (large photograph).

Some 500 kilometers (312 miles) west of Ulan Bator, in a side valley of the Urd Tamir River, on the northern flank of the Khangai massif, lies one of the most beautiful lakes of Mongolia, Lake Terkhiyn Tsagaan. Here, at a height of 2,060 meters (6,757 feet), nature wears splendid garments where green lakeshores alternate with picturesque mountainsides. A paradise for flora and fauna, where anglers find large stocks of perch for fishing.

Not far from this lake, the town of Tsetserleg ("garden"), with 15,000 inhabitants, is set in a wide rocky basin. Brightly painted houses sprawl up the slopes. Apartment blocks and well-cared

for parks alternate with arable land where barley is grown around the outskirts of the town. Originally founded as a monastery, Tsertserleg was turned into a secular settlement during the mid-1950s.

The monastery of Zayain Khüree survived the Cultural Revolution almost unscathed. Behind it, in the rock face of the mountain Bulgan Uul, which surrounds the town, a depiction of an old man wearing a white deel can be seen. The population still remembers with reverence this old and charitable man and honors him with Buddhist ceremonies and traditional ritual dances.

The rock picture, chiseled deep into the stone, even survived intact several attempts by the Chinese and Russian communists to destroy it.

In spite of Western influence on fashions, the coat-like deel, the traditional item of clothing of the Mongols, is still is worn by everyone – men and women, children and old people alike. Two buttons and eyelets are used to fasten the colorful coat, at the collar and under the right arm. The büs, a sash of cloth or silk three meters (10 feet) long and 25 centimeters (10 inches) wide, is wrapped around the deel at the hips.

See page 71

The outer wall of the Lamaist monastery of Erdene Zuu is adorned with 108 stupas.

The Capital of the Mongol Empire: Kharakhorum

Kharakhorum – Founded by Genghis Khan, Destroyed by the Chinese

Granite tortoises weighing several tonnes and a number of pillars recall the ancient Mongol capital city, Kharakhorum, which was destroyed by the Chinese in the 14th century.

Around 300 kilometers (188 miles) southwest of Ulan Bator, in a region known as Kharkhorin, lie the ruins of Kharakhorum. It was here, on the plain of a wide valley, where the Orkhon River flows out of the Eastern Khangai Mountains, that the construction of the magnificent city was begun in the year 1220, during the lifetime of Genghis Khan (1162–1227). It was, however, not completed until 1236, nine years after the death of the ruler.

The first regent of the empire was Genghis Khan's third son, Ögödei. As the "ruler of all rulers" he made Kharakhorum the political, economic and cultural center of the Mongol Empire that, at the zenith of its might, extended from the Pacific Ocean in the east to the Black Sea in the west. Kharakhorum, (the name means something like "black rock" or "black gravel") was constructed in a square measuring four by four kilometers (2.5 miles square), surrounded by a low wall. The spacious interior was a maze of streets and dwelling houses built of bricks. In the southwest of the capital city was Ögödei's palace with a roof of colored tiles resting on 64 wooden pillars eight meters (26 feet) high. These, in turn stood on a foundation made of large slabs of granite.

In its heyday, many ambassadors, scholars and merchants from Asia and Europe visited Kharakhorum, one of whom was the Franciscan monk William of Rubruck from the Flemish town of Rubrouck. He traveled from Constantinople to this area on foot, on horseback and in ox-drawn carts during the years 1253 to 1255. In his book "Journey to the Court of the Great Khan Mongke" he tells of his visit to the court of the ruler of the Mongols of that period, Mangu (or Mongke) Khan: "Not far from the city wall of Kharakhorum, Mongke has a large palace that, like our monasteries, is surrounded by a brick wall. There stands a huge palace in which, twice a year, the Khan holds a drinking session, normally around our Easter time when he travels though the region there, and again

in the summer when he is on the return journey. (…) The palace is constructed like a church. It has a central nave, and behind two rows of columns, two side naves, and at the southern end, three towers. (…) At the northern side, the Khan is seated on a raised

platform, so that he is visible to all present. (…) Regarding the city of Kharakhorum, (…) there are two districts; one is for the Saracens, where markets are held and many merchants congregate in order to be near the court, but also because of the envoys who stay here. And then, there is the district of the Cathays, who are mainly craftsmen. Beyond these districts are the large houses belonging to the secretaries employed by the court. The different peoples have twelve temples

for their idols, two mosques in which the teachings of Mohammed are proclaimed, and at the farthest end of the city a Christian church. The whole city is surrounded by a mud wall and has four gates. At the east gate, millet and other cereals are sold; however, these are very seldom imported here. At the western entrance, sheep and goats are on offer, at the southern entrance, oxen and wagons, and at the northern entrance, horses."

For only 24 years (from 1236 to 1260), Kharakhorum was the political and cultural center of the Mongols. Later, Kublai Khan transferred his residence to Beijing. Not until 1368, after the overthrow of the Yuan Dynasty by the Chinese people, did Kharakhorum once again become the capital of

the Mongol feudal state. However, after this, it decayed progressively, until the Chinese reached the land of origin of the Mongols in the year 1388 and razed Kharakhorum to the ground. In the year 1889, archeologists working in the valley plain of the Ork-

Archeologists at work in Kharakhorum: little by little, parts of the metropolis that was destroyed five hundred years ago are being uncovered.

hon River, first discovered the remains of the city. Thanks to the excavation work by German and Mongolian scientists in the past years, Kharakhorum has now been included in the UNESCO world cultural heritage list.

69

At the Khorgo Volcano: The Backdrop for a Science-Fiction Movie

Farther northwest, only a few kilometers from the idyllic setting of Lake Terkhiyn Tsagaan, lies a volcanic region that would make an ideal backdrop for a science-fiction movie. Between bizarrely-shaped lava flows and rugged rock formations, the cone of the extinct Khorgo volcano rises with its highest crater at a height of 2,240 meters (7,347 feet).

This volcano spewed out its fiery lava for the last time in 4000 BC. On the southern slopes of the former volcano one can still see the cooled lava bubbles, which can be up to 1.70 meters (5 feet 8 inches) high. The Mongols call the strange lava sculptures "stone yurts."

At the time of the eruption, a huge flow of lava blocked off a whole mountain valley on the Khorgo. This caused a body of water to collect that now is more than 55 square kilometers (21 square miles) in area and forms the 16-kilometer (10-mile) long Lake Terkhiyn Tsagaan. Here, mandarin ducks and cormorants have their nesting places, and anglers catch perch. Deer, boar and wild sheep inhabit the forests of larch and Swiss pines on the northern flank of the volcanic massif.

A Wise Man Travels Through the Khangai Mountains

Since ancient times, the mighty massif of the Mongolian Khangai Mountains has been considered an almost impassable barrier. In this natural world, shrouded in mystery, dotted with labyrinthine clefts in granite rocks formations, square Cyclopean boulders, green valleys and dusty, bleak depressions, many explorers and traveling merchants repeatedly met with disaster while searching for new discoveries and knowledge.

Many hundreds of years before Russia's scientists explored Mongolia in the name of the Czar, a group of Taoists traveled into the Khangai Mountains in the year 1221 and crossed this still unknown rocky territory. These settlers, Taoist philosophers and poets, were a strange little group that attempted to influence the world around them by leading a worthy lifestyle, as an example to others. The Taoists revered an invisible source of energy and, for example, compared death and life to cold and warmth. The origins of this religion date far back into pre-Christian times when it was a rival to Buddhism, which was developing at the time.

At Lake Terkhiyn Tsagaan, which was formed when the Khorgon volcano erupted, loneliness and silence prevail (left-hand page, top) – The crater of the Khorgon volcano appears dark and mysterious (left-hand page, bottom). – Paths and trails through the Khangai Mountains lead across old wooden bridges (below).

The rumor that Taoist monks were seeking ways of extending the human lifespan aroused the interest of Genghis Khan. Inspired by the hope of finding the secret of eternal life for himself, the Mongol ruler sent a messenger – with the following, authentically handed down request – to the 72-year-old Chang Chun, who was considered to be one of the most important Taoists of the 13th century.

"I (...), a dweller of the northern steppe, have no dissolute inclinations. I love simplicity and purity of customs, reject luxury and practice moderation. I wear the same robes as the horse herders and eat the same food. During seven years I accomplished great deeds and secured my power in all parts of the world. My position is high, the responsibilities are weighty, but I fear that my government is lacking in something. As, when one builds a ship, one equips it with a rudder, so as to cross over the rivers, I also invite wise men to me (...) I have not ceased to think

71

of you. Do not fear the wide steppe; come out of pity for the people, in their present situation, or at least out of mercy to me. Name a means to lengthen my life. I myself will wait for you."

Thus it came about that the modest scholar and poet, Chang Chun, a member of the sect of the "Golden Water Lily," set out on a long and dangerous journey. With some of his pupils he traveled with a caravan through the Khangai Mountains and followed the river Tuul Gol, one of the longest rivers in Mongolia, to the land of three rivers, where the Ider, Bugusi and Delgermurun unite to form the Selenge River.

Khangai Mountains: Beyond the yurts of the nomads, the wide, green grass steppes give way to rugged, snow-covered mountains (above). In spite of old traditions, motorization is finding its way into the Mongolian steppe. Besides heavily laden trucks,

automobiles jeeps or motor bikes, which are lovingly maintained and decorated, the horse is still the preferred traveling companion. In the case of a breakdown, a game of cards helps while away the time until help arrives (right-hand page).

The travelers of those days encountered severe difficulties and deprivation as they followed the winding paths that led across the Mongolian steppe, through dangerous salt marshes, over green hills and wind-swept mountain passes. The destination of the Tao hermits was the military camp of the famous Mongol ruler, beyond Amu Darya, south of the Hindu Kush Mountains.

The Desire for Immortality

After many weeks of traveling, the caravan of Chang Chun arrived at the shore of Buir Nuur, a lake in the steppe, rich in fish and eleven meters (36 feet) deep, where black storks and common spoonbills nest, and where the present border with China runs along the northwest shore. A brother of Genghis Khan had set up camp here with white yurts and welcomed the Taoists with all honors. The monks remained in Buir Nuur for sixteen days before continuing their journey to the camp of Genghis Khan, taking with them one hundred horses and oxen.

Li Chi Chang, a pupil of Chang Chun, who accompanied the elderly scholar through the empire of the Mongols, kept a diary of the Taoists' journey to the military camp of Genghis Khan. He called it "Hsi Yu Ki," or "The Journey to the West"; it was published in Russia in the "Publications of the Russian Spiritual Mission in Beijing" in 1866. In these narratives he tells of the exotic landscapes that repeatedly opened up to the Taoists, as they passed through the unknown land with their ox-drawn wagons.

"The journey led in winding paths through a hilly region. No matter where we came, everywhere we saw bands of salt on the land and pools with brackish water. The whole day long I did not meet a single traveler and perhaps once a year one might encounter a horse."

Finally they arrived at the camp of the Great Khan, who had the wise Chang Chun instruct him in the Taoist teachings. Many weeks filled with profound conversation followed, during which the conqueror and the monk felt drawn to one another, although Genghis Khan had to learn that there was no remedy to make him immortal. This news shocked the Mongol ruler – and indeed, made his conquests seem questionable to him.

Strangely, both Genghis Khan and Chang Chun died in August of the year 1227, long after their encounter. Genghis Khan fell during a campaign of conquest against the Xixia (Tangut) Empire. Mongolian warriors subsequently bore his body to his homeland and killed everyone they met along the way, so as to keep the news of his death and the site of his burial place secret.

Green meadows at the foot of the Khangai Mountains guarantee the nomads the survival of their herds of livestock (right). At a well in the Khangai Mountains, a shepherd draws bucketfuls of precious water from the depths (below).

Chang Chun, in contrast, died in the company of his pupils. The wise man was interred in a temple and the following words were chiseled on a stone slab there, words that the monk is once supposed to have spoken to Genghis Khan:

"Immortality requires neither medicine nor searching for secret invocations; of the true way to earn salvation this word alone is testimony – thou shalt not kill."

Khangai Mountains – a world of untouched nature.

The Power of Lamaism

The Erdene Zuu Monastery

1

1 and 2 Erdene Zuu: young novice monks on their way to lessons in the monastery, where Tibetan sutras and the scriptures of Lamaistic (Tibetan) Buddhism are taught.

2

Along the routes of the nomads and the caravans, Lamaism was introduced to the steppe regions of Mongolia – starting in the 15th century – and gradually replaced the shamanism that had previously been widespread among the Mongol nomads. It was Tsongkhapa (1356–1418) who reformed Buddhism in the Tibetan Ganden Monastery – and derived Lamaism from the Buddhist teaching of salvation.

It is a teaching that could be adapted to the needs of the nomadic peoples of the steppe and that taught its followers contemplation, and to despise passions and covetousness. With the spread of Lamaism, the Mongolian steppes of the warlike equestrian armies were transformed into a landscape of prayer wheels and monasteries. Furthermore, Lamaism gave a whole people a belief in a reward in a future life. At the center of the teaching is the belief in the re-birth of human beings, who must experience many lives on this earth before the soul finds salvation and liberation.

Two great champions of Lamaism were the Mongol feudal princes, Altan Khan from the Tumet tribe in southern Mongolia and Abadai Khan from the Khalkha tribe in northern Mongolia. In the late 16th century, after a lengthy journey to Tibet, Abadai Khan built the monastery of Erdene Zuu, from which the Lamaist religion spread to the whole of Mongolia. Constructed on the site of the ancient capital of Kharakhorum, the monastery became not only the religious center of Lamaism, but also the focal point of the territory ruled by Abadai Khan.

The famous Lamaist monastic complex of Erdene Zuu (meaning approximately "precious sanctuary" or "precious lord") was built in the year 1586 in one section of the extensive ruins of Kharakhorum, the former Mongolian capital. It is the oldest Lamaist monastery on Mongolian territory and, with

3

an area of 400 by 400 meters (1,312 feet square), is surrounded by a wall that is visible from afar.

An eye-catching feature of this wall are the 108 stupas, placed at regular intervals, that were erected to commemorate historical events or in honor of worldly or spiritual dignitaries. Most of the monastic complex was built by the Mongol master architect, Mandshir, and the numerous temples and pagodas that are decorated with fascinating sculptures and colorful paintings are regarded as an important cultural monument of the Mongolian people.

Today, Erdene Zuu is a monastic museum, known far beyond the borders of the country, where the temples and prayer houses hold unique cultural and historic collections. A further attraction is the restored main building of the monastery, which contains more than 1,700 statues of Buddha. Not less impressive is the virtually pyramid-shaped white building of the suburgan. The blunt conical tip, adorned with thirty metal rings, is not only crowned with the symbols of the sun and the moon, but also with a blazing flame – the symbol of wisdom.

4

3 Services of worship are held regularly in the magnificent interior of the monastery, with its golden Buddha figures.

4 The monks at the monastery wear red robes.

Dwelling Places of Gods, Spirits and Demons

The Mountains of the Mongolian Altai and Gobi-Altai

"Holy places never had a beginning. They were holy from the moment of their discovery, drew their existence from the breath of unseen presences. Human beings sense their invisible radiance with fear or amazement, and religions, which fall to their knees in their human weakness when confronted with the inexplicable, seek names and symbols for the inexplicable."
Giuseppe Tucci, *Land of Snows*

No sound can be heard, not a single movement perceived. It is like the creation of the world, when nothing yet existed. A silence that is not only peaceful and reassuring, but which also confronts one with the complete absence of any kind of noise. A silence that almost makes one dizzy. Even more than that: gazing at the wild, archaic landscape, the feeling of timelessness is not only intensified as our gaze sweeps across rock domes, bizarre canyons, and weird stone terraces that are millions of years old; here one can also feel as if one has been transported back in time to a period that is not so distant, when people projected innumerable gods, spirits and demons into the labyrinths of the Altai Mountains.

Here, in western Mongolia, nature has created sky-high fortresses and temples of stone, where enormous arenas of rock were formed from oceans of boulders layered on top of each other, and where rugged mountain aeries alternate with huge stone palaces, some of which are barely accessible to our immediate awareness. Everything appears foreign – and yet enchants us. Perhaps it is because here, supernatural beings dwell in the

Offering at an ovoo: at a crossroads in the Altai Mountains, the skull of a sheep has been left as a sacrificial offering (above). – Young Kazakh boy with a fur cap (right).

When the shadows lengthen in the Altai Mountains, dung patties or firewood will be placed on the fire in the stove in the yurts. Trails of smoke then rise into the air, while sheep and goats gather around the house tent (right-hand page).

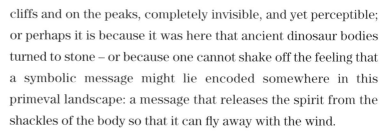

cliffs and on the peaks, completely invisible, and yet perceptible; or perhaps it is because it was here that ancient dinosaur bodies turned to stone – or because one cannot shake off the feeling that a symbolic message might lie encoded somewhere in this primeval landscape: a message that releases the spirit from the shackles of the body so that it can fly away with the wind.

That is how a traveler may feel after climbing one of the numerous high passes of the Altai Mountains, while taking a contemplative rest beside an ovoo. Ovoo is the name given to a pile of rough stones, which is considered to be the dwelling of local deities or spirits. Wooden poles or branches on which colored lengths of cloth are hung project from it.

At these natural memorials, where shamanism has long outlived the decline of the Mongol Empire, the spirits of the mountains and trails are still honored with sacrificial offerings, such as a stone from along the path; a piece of white cheese; some flour, millet or tea. One also gives thanks to the local spirit beings for the successful journey by saying a prayer and circling the ovoo three times, asking for further protection, while every time they flutter, the ragged prayer flags distribute their blessings with the wind

Do spirits and gods of happiness or powers of darkness really dwell here? The only certain thing is: in the mountainous Altai the supernatural is still omnipresent, and in the presence of the bare rocky labyrinth between vertical cliff walls, dark gorges and narrow ridges, the veil between reality and that which exists beyond becomes more transparent than in other places.

The Longest Mountain Range in Mongolia

The main range of the Mongolian Altai and the Gobi Altai stretches for some 1,700 kilometers (1,063 miles) across Mongolia – from the northwest to the south. It is a vast complex of mountain ranges, the longest and highest range in Mongolia.

The characteristic feature of the Mongolian Altai (Altyn Nuru) is the continuity of the main ridge, a feature that is lacking in the Gobi Altai. The latter consist instead of individual, isolated

Left-hand page: In the evening, the goats return from the meadow to Ulgii (top). – Traveling by canoe through the foaming waters of the Khovd Gol (center). Friends wearing the traditional deel meet on a bench to exchange the latest news (bottom). Right-hand page: The north of Mongolia is covered with dense forest (right, top). – Main square of the town of Ulgii in the Altai Mountains (center). – Kazakh graves with the rocky snow-covered Altai Mountains in the background (bottom right).

mountain massifs or ranges that are separated by wide, deep depressions.

The Empire of Glaciers

The Mongolian Altai begin in northwestern Mongolia, where the borders of Russia, China and Mongolia meet, and where a junction of mountain ranges forms the striking Tavan Bogd Group. They separate from the Russian Altai and extend first of all to the southeast before making a sweeping curve southwards and then finally continuing eastwards.

The main ridge of the Mongolian Altai, formed by several mountain ranges merging close together, runs for about 1,000 kilometers (625 miles) as a unbroken range. The steep ridges or rounded summits of the northwest Altai are mainly covered with ice and snow, especially Khuiten, which at a height of 4,374

84

meters (14,347 feet) is the highest peak in Mongolia. Only a few trails at heights of 3,000 meters (9,840 feet) cross the saddles of this rugged range, where the scenery is breathtaking and nature presents the divine in tangible forms.

In the northwestern Mongolian Altai there are more than 100 glaciers. The largest of them lie in remote mountain massifs with mysterious names: Munk-Khairkhan (4,231 m/13,878 ft), Turgen Kharkhira (3,965 m/13,005 ft) and Tavan Bogd (4,374 m/14,347 ft). In the latter we find the Potanin Glacier, which was named for the famous Russian explorer of Asia. With a length of about twenty kilometers (12.5 miles), this ice sheet is the most important glacier in Mongolia.

The extensive signs of glaciation on the main ridge are mainly a result of the long winters and the high altitudes. In addition, the high regions of the Mongolian Altai are exposed to cold west and northwest winds that even in the summer months occasionally

The life of the nomads in the wide expanses of the Altai Mountains is determined by their herds of live-stock: yaks are slaughtered, sheep washed in the river, or the hooves of horses shod.

Hans Leder –
A Collector of Insects in the Mongol Empire

The natural scientist and ethnologist Hans Leder (1843–1921) set out from Ulan Bator with a caravan in 1891 to travel to the Sayan Mountains in order to collect insects, after which he continued his journey farther into the inaccessible interior of the country. Leder, who was born in Jauernig in the region formerly known as Austrian Silesia, was motivated primarily by curiosity and a fondness of travel to explore, first Algeria, then the Atlas Mountains, the Sahara and finally Caucasia, where he discovered previously unknown species of insect.

His discoveries finally led the scientist, who lived in Mödling near Vienna, to Mongolia on a commission from the Russian Geographical Society Not far from the monastery Erdene Zuu in the center of Mongolia, he became the first to discover a long-forgotten site of ruins. He had found the remains of the old capital city of the Uyghurs, along with "mani" stones with inscriptions and derelict irrigation systems.

Leder fell in love with the Mongol culture and particularly during his second journey (1899/1900) he purchased thousands of precious items: fragments of Lamaist texts, scroll paintings and miniatures, clay plaques (tsatsa), as well as figures made of metal and paper mache.

Hans Leder's collections, which "in total consisted of more than 20,000 numbered and precisely described items" are now spread among many museums and have made a significant contribution to our knowledge of Mongolia.

bring snow, which is then blown across the rocky ridges. There, in the lee of the northeast and eastern slopes, it often lies and accumulates, causing much more favorable conditions for the formation of glaciers than in the other regions.

Impressive traces of former glacial activity can still be clearly recognized in the high massif of the Altai Mountains. In wide cirques or broad, flat valleys of the higher regions, these effects are just as noticeable as in the steep gorges where rapid mountain streams flow. In many places these rivers have retained the character of the glacial valley, and the valley bottom is often strewn with rugged boulders.

In the splendid solitude of the Altai Mountains, where herds of livestock graze and the yurts of the shepherds stand near a meandering river, humans have already made their mark: numerous trails carve up the countryside like knife-marks.

In addition to the steep cliffs separated by valleys and depressions, the slopes of the Mongolian Altai often feature mountain forest and mountain steppe. Especially the slopes beyond the watershed have much denser vegetation than those in the inner areas of the mountains, where there is predominantly steppe vegetation. But the farther one follows this range of mountains in a southeasterly direction, the more arid it becomes.

The dry regions of the Mongolian Altai are also the reason for the very sparse population in these areas. Only in places where mountain steppe and alm-like meadows provide good pastureland for their livestock, does one find the nomads traveling with their herds in the mountains.

In the northwest of Mongolia, in particular, various nomadic tribes have since earliest times maintained a special kind of cultivation, while following a lifestyle with a migratory pattern in several phases. After working in the fields, the nomads migrate up into the Altai in spring, returning in the late summer months to gather in the harvest. Then they seek a suitable place to spend the winter in their transportable yurts. When the ice and snow have gone, they return to the start at the fertile fields.

Nonetheless, northwestern Mongolia is one of the poorest areas of the country. The high rates of unemployment have for many years been driving increasing numbers of Kazakhs (Sunni Muslims), who make up a large proportion of the population here, back to the land their ancestors came from. In contrast to the Mongolians, the Kazakhs live in larger yurts that have much steeper roofs. Moreover, they love bright colors – a passion they demonstrate both in their yurts and in their clothing. In 1940, the Kazakh national aimag (province) of Bayan-Ulgii was created specifically for them.

A Ram's Horn as a Sacrifice

The animal world of the Mongolian Altai is truly varied, in spite of the extreme climate. Besides the snow leopard, which inhabits all the alpine regions, whether in the eternal snows or in the desert steppe, there is also the ibex, Altai ibex, and wild sheep, also called *argali* in Mongolia. Male animals of this species can measure 125 centimeters (4 feet 2 inches) at the withers and weigh up to 200 kilograms (440 pounds). The large spiral-shaped ram horns are occasionally found as sacrificial offerings at the ovoos, those windblown piles of rock that guard the mountain passes and are thought to be the dwelling of local deities and spirits.

Pipe-smoking is very popular with Mongolian women as they get older (above).
Right-hand page: In order to reach another location for the camp, a nomad family crosses the Khovd Gol. Camels and goats must be brought across the river, as well as all the household items. Some parts are towed across the river on floating truck tires (right-hand page). In front of a yurt all the members of a Tuva camp assemble for a group photograph (right-hand page, center).

See page 94

In the Tent Homes of the Mongols

Life in the Yurt

Since earliest times, the yurt has been the traditional dwelling of the Turkic and Mongol peoples. The first Mongol yurt, with latticed walls covered with felt, dates from the 6th century AD, according to Chinese sources. Later, European travelers described and drew pictures of the Mongolian yurt in their many publications; they were fascinated by this type of mobile accommodation, especially the large palace yurts, which could not be dismantled and were placed on wheels to be pulled by draft animals from one place to the next.

The yurt is still the ideal dwelling for the nomadic life in the steppe and the desert. Easily transported by a few camels, the round tent with a conical roof can be dismantled and provides a safe shelter from extremes of weather. The erection and furnishing of the yurt does not generally take much longer than half a day, meaning that the nomads are able to change their location relatively quickly.

The Mongolians call their movable dwelling a *ger* (a term which refers to all types of house), although the name "yurt" is much more frequently used by Euro-

Living according to ancient tradition: wherever there is adequate fodder and water for the nomads' livestock, their yurts are erected – round, portable house tents made of wooden lattices and poles, felt mats, fabric and with a wooden door. In the cozy interior, where the beds are also placed, decorative, colorful carpets and pictures adorn the walls. – Yurts of the Kazakh people at the river Khovd Gol in the Altai Mountains (right-hand page, center).

Seeking grass and water, the nomads of Mongolia have been on the move with their animals since early times. Their path leads through the wide steppes where neither houses nor any other kind of trail marker can be found along the way. Only here and there in the valleys stand the round white dwellings – yurts – of the animal herders. Their shape is ideally adapted to the nature of the land.

the felt covers become dirty over time. In addition, a square flap of canvas is fastened to the yurt roof, so that in bad weather the open roof hole can be closed with a cord.

The size of the yurt depends on the number of lattice walls used; normally the diameter is between three and six meters (9.8 and 19.6 feet). Under the open roof ring it is not quite three meters (9.8 feet) high and at the outer walls only

peans. Its origin is found in the Turkic word *jurt* that means something like tent, camp site, dwelling place or home.

The basic framework of a simple Mongolian yurt consists of several wooden latticed walls that resemble folding fencing, which, when they are extended, can be set up in a circular form before being tied together with horsehair. The wooden poles of each section of lattice are held together by small leather nails that have a minute head to prevent them falling out.

The door of the yurt is placed on the south side of the circular tent (the direction that is sacred to the Mongolians), between two sections of the latticed structure. Then two ropes are bound around the circular construction of the lattice work and fastened to the door posts. The roof poles are now placed on the V-shaped ends of the lattice poles and lashed firmly with cords; at the top, the

long roof poles are fitted into a wooden smoke-ring on the outer side of which matching grooves have been hollowed out. The various types of smoke ring serve as a symbol of the ethnic identity of the tribe. In addition, the dome-shaped wooden roof is supported by two wooden pillars.

After this, the roof and lattice walls are covered with felt. The thickness of the felt covering depends on the weather. In summer, the felt cover is folded up half a meter, so that the cooling winds can blow through the yurt. In winter, on the other hand, when the nomads need shelter from the cold, the yurt frame is usually covered with three to five layers of felt that are secured with ropes of camel hair.

As a more recent development, a white canvas cover is normally spread over the felt as protection against moisture. This canvas cover is easy to wash, whereas

1.2 to 1.5 meters (4 to 5 feet). At the center of the yurt is the fire or stove, and smoke is led out by a stove pipe through the roof ring.

The threshold has a ritual function; it protects the interior from evil spirits. Even the earliest travelers reported that stepping on the threshold was strictly forbidden. And modern-day Mongolians still believe that anyone who stumbles over the threshold of a yurt brings bad luck.

91

The valley of Khovd Gol in the Altai Mountains.

Where the Mongolian Altai Lose Height

A bird's eye view of the Mongolian Altai as they run southwards reveals several parallel ranges lying to the east of the main ridge, characterized by huge dome-shaped cliffs, steep slopes and crevices, and scree fields and granite boulders. One of these impressive high ranges is the Dartsag Khuren (2,656 m/8,712 ft), which runs towards the northwest and joins the mighty ridge of the Sotai. The third link in this chain is the elongated Bayr Nuru with the snowy peak of Churu Undur rising to 3,675 meters (12,054 feet).

It is striking that the almost continuous main range of the Mongolian Altai increasingly loses in height as it extends in a southeasterly direction. The gigantic mountains that rise to enormous heights gradually disappear, and the mountains then fall below 3,000 meters (9,840 ft) and then, finally, below the 2,000-meter (6,560 ft) mark. Their rugged crests also become flatter and take on the form of high plateaus that are only occasionally dominated by Cyclopean peaks.

The easternmost point of the Mongolian Altai is marked by Ederengen Nuru. Although it is 2,042 meters (6,698 ft) high, it barely rises 600 meters (1,968 ft) above the surrounding area.

Located in a very barren and dry region, it is therefore considered by many of the nomads to form part of the desert-like mountains of the Gobi Altai.

The Gobi Altai

In southeastern Mongolia, where the ranges of the Gobi Altai descend towards the Gobi Desert, elongated mountain ranges and isolated massifs, separated by wide depressions, form a fascinating landscape. Many of the expansive elevated areas of the Gobi Altai retain the same plateau-like character of the Mongolian Altai.

The highest peak of the Gobi Altai is Ikh Bogd, also known as Baruun Bogd, which reaches a height of more than 4,000 meters (13,120 feet). Even birch and aspen trees grow in its numerous crevices and gorges. Equally impressive is Baga Bogd (3,554 m/ 11,657 ft). It is shaped like a majestic dome with steep, inaccessible slopes. And then there is the stately range of the Arza Bogd. This is an elongated massif, the highest point of which is Ikh Bayan (2,453 m/8,046 ft). As well as trees and scrub, juniper (arza) also grows in the valleys here and gave the mountains their name.

The largest part of the Gobi Altai does not invoke harmony or contemplation, but rather destruction and chaos. Here there are

At a small river in the Altai Mountains, where some yurts stand, the sky turns pink and violet. Evening light touches the earth and transforms the landscape at Khar Us Nuur with glowing power (below and right-hand page).

is the large fluctuations in temperatures between day and night and between summer and winter. Especially during the hot summer months, one can often hear the blocks of stone bursting apart and cracking. Then the power of erosion is awe-inspiring as it demonstrates to us how large rocks slide down into the valley, as if glaciers of stone were extending down from the mountainous heights.

Thus, more and more of the mountains are being buried under their own detritus, called *belj* by the Mongolians. This rock debris extends to form large foothill plains that demonstrate all the typical features of desert erosion.

Belj are also considered a characteristic feature of the Gobi Altai. Near the mountain at the head of the valleys they consist of coarse scree. The greater the distance from the mountain, the smaller are the pieces of rock debris, which are sometimes reminiscent of broken roof tiles and slide into long valleys that the Mongolians call *saire*. There the heaps of stone finally disintegrate completely: this is the transformation of stone into sand.

As a result of the arid climate, the flora and fauna of the Gobi Altai are not very varied. Apart from some poor vegetation cover, there are scarcely any plants. And the animal world does not boast a wide range of species, but is more typical of desert regions. Furthermore, there are neither continually flowing watercourses, nor any other body of water worth mentioning, although many traces indicate that in the dry hollows of this area there were once several lakes.

Apart from the great aridity, that in southeastern Mongolia doubtless exceeds the tolerable limits for most life forms, this region is also very susceptible to earthquakes. The highlands of the Gobi Altai and the valleys of the Gobi lakes to the north – elongated depressions with salt and freshwater lakes that have no outlet and are separated from each other by low ridges – have always been known to be tectonically instable. In November 1957 there were such severe tremors in the earth's crust that in spite of the sparse population in this remote corner of the world, the number of victims was very large.

Moreover, in recent years the Gobi Altai have become particularly famous for the numerous discoveries of fossils from the Cretaceous period. In layers that are many millions of years old, scientists have discovered almost completely preserved skeletons of carnivorous dinosaurs. The remains of herbivorous dinosaurs and other animals that inhabited the Gobi Altai and also the Central Gobi desert during the Cretaceous period are also spectacular. It forms a unique wonderland of paleontology.

no feelings of well-being; no views of esthetic beauty to enjoy. Beautifully-formed shapes and imposing sculptures are rare. Instead, this region seems like something from a distant planet, where vast rocky landscapes continually explode in the course of long geological periods, under the influence of the enormous fluctuations in temperature.

Almost everywhere, the dynamic forces of erosion are at work, and these guarantee that the mountains of the Gobi Desert are anything but a rigid, uniform landscape. The fascination of this furrowed world, in spite of all barrenness, is omnipresent. It is scarcely possible to escape the magic of this inhospitable landscape. At the sight of the mountains – across parched earth and land baked by the sun – the traveler is more than rewarded for all the difficulties endured on the journey from Ulan Bator to this far-away world of stone. Here, massive and defiant mountain forms alternate with gorge-like valleys and scree deltas.

The principal cause of the erosion of rocks in the Gobi Altai

Altai Mountains: Landscape of cliffs and ice at Tavan Bogd.

Hunting with Eagle and Shotgun

How the Mongolians Hunt Bears and Marmots

1 The Kazakhs hunt with trained eagles. 2 and 5 In the north of Mongolia, a married couple display a collection of historical firearms in front of their block house.

Since time immemorial, hunting has played a significant role in the life of the Mongolian people. Even in the Stone Age, they chiefly found nourishment by hunting. And Temüjin himself, who later became Genghis Khan, and his siblings found food when they were young by hunting marmots and field mice. The famous Franciscan monk, Giovanni de Plano Carpini, who traveled as papal envoy to visit the Mongol Great Khan Guyuk, a grandson of Genghis Khan, in his palace at Kharakhorum in the years 1245 and 1246, reported that the Mongols ate almost nothing other than what they had hunted.

For many centuries the Mongols have hunted as individual hunters or in a group, holding large battues in which whole tribes participated. The prey was then divided up so that everyone received a share according to their social status.

They hunted with lances and with bows and arrows; later with firearms and strychnine (for hunting wolves). Many kinds of trap are still also used today, as well as the urga, a kind of lasso on a long pole. Even eagles – with a wingspan of nearly two meters (6.6 feet) and weighing up to five kilograms – are trained by the Mongols for the hunt. And furthermore, bird whistles or trained dogs are frequently used, usually from the saddle of a horse or a motor vehicle.

Today the land of Genghis Khan still has an abundance of animals that can be hunted. The one that is hunted most intensively is the Mongolian or Siberian marmot (steppe marmot) (Marmota bobac sibirica) and the Altai (gray) marmot (Marmota bobac baibacina), both of which inhabit the steppe, mountain forest steppe and sub-alpine elevations of the high mountains. The fur of this rodent, which lives exclusively on plants, is of excellent quality and a much sought-after export commodity.

The meat of the marmot is considered a special delicacy. A recipe from olden times is still appreciated today: the meat is drawn out through the gullet of the marmot and the bones are removed. The meat is then seasoned with wild onions and salt and stuffed back into the skin, tied at the neck opening and lightly roasted in the fire or boiled in water. It is a favorite meal when out hunting.

100

Because it is a danger to domesticated animals, the wolf is hunted all year round – without any close season. The main hunting season, however, is the winter, when its grey fur is thickest. In some years, up to 5,000 animals are killed. Squirrels and foxes were exploited in even greater numbers for their fur. In the past, more than 100,000 were killed each year. Now, however, these animals are protected – at certain seasons of the year – by a ban on shooting them. These close seasons also apply to deer and wild goats. There are even more severe hunting restrictions for ermine, polecat, lynx, and marten. Bears may be shot only in certain numbers each year and only with a permit. And the Gobi bear, stone marten, wild camel, wild donkey, wild sheep, ibex, reindeer, elk, saiga antelope, snow leopard, fish otter, and sable have for many decades been under strict protection.

3 and 4 In the Altai Mountains, where hunters occasionally wear an ammunition belt around their wrist, the Mongolians primarily hunt marmots.

4

5

3

Asia's Sea of Sand

The Gobi Desert

"*The landscape through which we are marching is, with all its bleak loneliness and poverty, one of the most magnificent that I know of in Asia. It is full of defiance and pride. With its rigid features, it gazes scornfully at us transient worms who have dared to venture into its paralyzing, terrible barrenness. (...) But at night, when we lie in our tent and listen to the silence of the darkness and the loneliness, then we may feel safe – we have everything with us that we need – but in reality, we are resting on unsafe ground. We are totally dependent on the camels, the 'ships of the desert' that have borne us into the forbidden land and without which we could never leave it again alive. Everything depends on their health and wellbeing. If they should fail, we are lost – like people on a ship that is shipwrecked.*

Over the date September 16, a shimmer of mysticism, of fairytales and of eternity seemed to hover, an atmosphere that was anything but mundane. We took another step deeper into the monstrous Gobi Desert ..."
Sven Hedin, *Across the Gobi Desert*

The sand dunes of Mongol Els, with an area of 2,724 square kilometers (1,051 square miles), are one of the largest areas of sand in Mongolia. The Zavkhan river forms the northernmost boundary of the ocean of sand. The lake of Dorgon Nuur (above). The faces of many inhabitants of the Gobi are weathered by the extreme desert climate (right).

Right-hand page: In the wide expanses of the desert, the gnarled branches of the saxaul bushes have been formed into bizarre shapes by the wind.

Gobi – even the name has a hint of secrecy and adventure. One thinks of endless oceans of grass and steppe, of sand dunes shaped by the wind and romantic nights by the light of a full moon. This desert is not bleak, but magical. Almost a paradise. But in paradise there are trees and bushes that are lacking here, and for a desert, the Gobi really has too much grass.

The traveler here is captivated by a landscape that has no beginning and no end. An arena that is both fascinating and hostile and that bears no comparison to anything else.

The Gobi is still considered the largest desert in Central Asia, stretching in a variety of forms and colors from the south and southwest of Mongolia to northern China. Nevertheless, the Mongolian part of the Gobi is more steppe-like semi-desert than true desert. This is because of the strong fluctuations in the cyclonic

summer rains that in a wide diversity of regions ensure thick grass cover and steppes carpeted with flowers.

These annual amounts of precipitation are, thus, also the reason why huge herds of horses could become established in this remote corner of the world. And that is why it is the cradle of a people, which about 800 years ago – under the leadership of the legendary Genghis Khan – conquered a world empire and, for a time, ruled an area from the Yellow Sea to Silesia.

The Inhabitants of the Gobi Desert

At no period in the past did the splendid Gobi play a significant role in Mongol or Chinese history. Neither epic poems, nor cosmographic or religious texts tell us anything about the lives of the early inhabitants of the desert. Maybe this is because there never was a united people of the desert. Rather, the dwellers of the Gobi consisted of numerous tribes of varying origins. They lived scattered in clans or founded small oasis cities, where they con-

structed clever irrigation systems, so as to live from the desert, in spite of its modest commercial potential.

Not until the heyday of the Silk Road (420–1400), when ever larger caravans passed through the Gobi, a corridor many hundreds of kilometers in width, did tiny supply stations develop into powerful desert cities – melting pots of different peoples with skin colors ranging from ivory to bronzed brown.

For example, we could mention the Wusun, the ancestors of the Kazakhs; then the Yuezhi, Tocharians, Xianbi, Rouran and Western Xia (Tanguts). But most significant were the Uyghurs, the descendents of Turko-Tatar tribes who, according to legend, had already ruled wide areas of the Gobi when the desert was still a fruitful paradise with wide rivers and legendary cities.

It is historical fact that the Uyghurs left their original home to the south of Lake Baikal in the 8th century and founded an empire in the steppe in present-day Mongolia – and in neighboring regions – and that during this time, they adopted first Manichaeism, through which they were led to Buddhism, until they were finally converted to Islam.

Even in the period of the powerful Tang and Yuan Dynasties, the Uyghurs dominated agriculture at the southern edge of the Gobi, where they cultivated cotton, vegetables, fruit and wheat. In their urge for self-determination and independence, they increasingly took up arms and resisted the domination of the Chinese. Today, Uyghur men can easily be spotted at the markets of many oasis cities; they usually wear three-quarter-length coats, high leather boots and fur hats or the traditional doppa (brightly colored cap).

Arvaykheer
Erdenedalay
Delgerzogt
Ayrag
EAST GOBI
Dariganga
GANGA NUUR
NATURE RESERVE
Naran
Mandal Gobi
Tugrug
Saykhan Owoo
MIDDLE GOBI
Undurschil
Ar Saynshand
HANGAI
Saynshand
INNER MONGOLIA
Uldsiit
Zuunbajan
Erdene
Zogt Ovoo
Mandakh
Bulgan
Manlay
Ulaan
Badrach
Zamyn Uud
Khuvsgul
Tsogt Tsetsi
Bayandalay
Dalandsadgad
Khatanbulag
Khanbogd
Noyon
SOUTH GOBI
Bajan Ovoo

CHINA

G o b i   D e s e r t

RUSSIA
MONGOLIA
CHINA

The counterpart to the Uyghurs – in their culture and clothing – are the Mongolian nomads, who are strongly influenced by Lamaism, a branch of Buddhism that was introduced to Mongolia from Tibet. In their long deel (overall, coat) which is tied with a yellow or green sash, the Mongols travel through the steppe and semi-desert with their herds of livestock during the brief, hot summer, always searching for good grazing land. Their everyday life has barely changed for centuries; they move their yurts almost weekly until the beginning of the long, cold winter, when they set up a permanent camp.

In the Realm of the Mongolian-Chinese Gobi

Even in the 21st century, the name "Gobi" is a word that still conjures up the fascination and danger of the unknown. On the map it resembles an elliptical body with an average length (from west to east) of approximately 2,000 kilometers (1,250 miles). The Mongolian-Chinese border runs almost exactly through the middle of this region, a line that divides the Gobi into two equally fascinating halves.

On the one side, in the Mongolian part, pale green grassland transitions into grey-brown steppe that finally becomes a large desert area of yellowish-red hues, with only a few scattered oases. And on the Chinese side, plains of rock detritus and scree alternate with cliff formations that are millions of years old and reach towards the sky to heights of more than 4,000 meters/ 13,120 feet (Karlik Shan, 4,925 m/16,154 ft); in between there are

A herd of camels in the southern Gobi, where the dunes of Khongor Els, a range of sand dunes, stretches for about 180 kilometers (113 miles). The waves of sand piled up by the wind reach heights of up to 30 meters (98 feet) (left-hand page, top). – A Mongol child sitting in front of a small shop (bottom).

Some yurts offer desert travelers a pleasant place to rest. Children in the Gobi Desert fetch water in a bucket.

105

vast areas with sand dunes, shaped into sickle forms by the wind and up to 300 meters (984 feet) in height.

The Mongolian part of the Gobi begins about 600 kilometers (375 miles) south of the capital Ulaanbaatar, with the most typical desert regions being located to the south of the Mongolian Altai and the Gobi Altai, in the Trans-Altai Gobi. Here the annual precipitation seldom amounts to more than 50 millimeters (2 inches), with the result that the region is almost totally uninhabited. Only around the sources of the streams, which usually quickly seep away, are there small oases that delight the eye with their lush vegetation – aspen trees, tamarisks and thickets of reeds.

But where the feather grass steppe becomes more and more arid and merges into the desert steppe that covers about 30 percent of the country, the vegetation cover disappears almost completely. Then, only isolated grasses, tumbleweed or tuft-like plants, some

with large thorns, are found. Here, the Gobi becomes a hostile desert where people – from horizon to horizon – feel like tiny ants.

There are Many Gobis

Without the local knowledge of a nomad, a stranger would never be able to find the way out of the depths of the Gobi desert, a place that lends a new dimension to all human activity and desire, and of which the Mongol name means approximately "large tub" or "flat basin."

For the native Mongolian and Chinese, there are even several "Gobis." for example, the "Black Gobi," where stony plains and dark, glittering scree covers the surface; then there is the "Red Gobi," dissected by crusted and furrowed earth; and, finally, the "Yellow Gobi," that is also called "Shamo." In this region of the desert, bizarrely-shaped sand dunes stretch towards the horizon.

107

Where Reality and Dreams Merge

The extreme and rapid changes in weather between day and night cause general destruction in the endless spaces of the Gobi Desert. In winter, cold air accumulates in the hollows, allowing temperatures to fall below minus 40° Celsius (-40° Fahrenheit). In July, on the other hand, the mercury can rise to over 45°C (113 ° Fahrenheit), causing the layers of air close to the ground to heat up.

While breaking horses in the corral and giving them water, the Mongols have the smell of horse sweat in their noses (above). – A recently-married Mongol man happily poses in his mobile house of wood and felt for a photograph with his wife, child and weapon (right-hand page).

In many places this leads to dangerous mirages in which fantasy and reality merge – moments in which the fata morgana build up my hopes of shimmering water or unruly lakes, the banks of which, however, I would never have reached. For those glittering waters that lay before me in the dusty valley basins were nothing other than reflections of the blue sky in the heat haze of the layers of air close to the ground.

Gobi – the "Wind Chamber" of Asia

Since ancient times the Gobi has been the home of the wind and of the spirits. In the roaring gusts of wind, billions of grains of sand hiss and beat against the crumbling cliffs, causing the traveler to think he is hearing the sounds of many different instruments: flutes, organs and violins. These are the songs of the wind, which make one believe they are the voices of spirits, and the nomads around their campfire fear their power.

In spring, especially, the wind is unceasing. It is the windiest season in Mongolia; there are almost no calm days then. Often there are dangerous storms with gale-force winds, roaring in from a westerly and northwesterly direction and lasting several days. During such a storm visibility can be reduced to only 50 meters (164 feet).

The storms race across the land with gale strengths from eight to twelve and destroy everything that lies in their path. Those who have not experienced a spring storm like this themselves, can scarcely imagine the violent power of nature that is revealed, transforming the Gobi into an arena of screaming noise.

On his last expedition, the Swedish explorer, Sven Hedin (1865–1952) experienced the absolute frenzy of an unpredictable Gobi storm at first hand, while he was crossing Asia's largest desert from Peking to Urumqi with camels in the winter of 1927/28 – a distance of 2,100 kilometers (1,313 miles). Like a dark wall, the sandstorm suddenly approached from the west; "… a thrilling, almost frightening sight," as Sven Hedin relates in one of his many books. "The sky was completely darkened by the myriad sand grains and dust particles. Fortunately I had already taken my bearings from the mountains in the north on the previous afternoon, for now it was as if they were obliterated and completely invisible. Mento came rushing in to me to secure a rope from the smoke ring to the floor in the interior of my yurt, which was then anchored to a few heavy packing cases outside. If they had been blown away, we might never have been able to recover them. Not to speak of my moveable property, that of

See page 115

Longing for Open Spaces and Mobility

Everyday Life of the Gobi Nomads

Over the centuries, the nomads of the Gobi remained largely unaffected by the many revolts that shook the Mongol people. During the 70 years of the communist era, as well as herding their own animals, they cared for the herds of the cooperatives which were obliged to supply many Mongolian towns as well as the former Soviet Union.

Now the inhabitants of the Gobi once again work to provide for their own families and keep large quantities of meat and milk for themselves, as the Mongolian currency, the tugrik (MNT) lacks stability.

Today, the livestock farming of the inhabitants of the Mongolian steppe still provides a valuable counterbalance to the arable farmers of northern China, where the wide sand and gravel plains of the Gobi merge into dry, short grass steppe. By means of irrigation systems, many regions of the Gobi have been made cultivable in order to produce rice, millet, wheat, grapes, melons and cotton.

At the same time, politicians in Ulan Bator and Beijing – much to the chagrin of the nomadic population – have for decades been pushing for the extraction of raw materials in the desert regions. Many families from the Gobi were cleverly enticed into the cities, where the nomads or farmers, however, only temporarily succumbed to the temptations of the modern age. Above all, the high rate of unemployment and loss of identity caused them much disappointment.

In addition, the nomadic families suffered badly from the air pollu-

1–3 Before the felt covers are placed over the wooden lattice walls of the yurts, the furniture, chests, beds and stove are set in their places. Sometimes the shepherds even have a satellite dish. – 4/5 The patient and undemanding "ship of the desert," that sometimes can be extremely stubborn, is an important working animal that can carry very heavy loads on its back or pull a cart with pneumatic tires. – 6 In the spacious interior of the yurt, children breakfast on boorsog, little cakes fried in fat, which they dip in their tea.

2

3

4

5

6

frugal, nomadic life – in spite of industrialization and the exploitation of mineral resources, as well as the increasing prevalence of television, that is spreading even into the desert. The chopping down of the saxaul bushes for fuel has also played a role, causing many lakes to dry out and oases to die.

In order to solve some of these controversial issues, the "Gobi Movement" was founded to fight for the protection of this unique desert landscape in Mongolia. With the support of the United Nations and other international organizations, the "Great Gobi National Park" was created, consisting of the Trans-Altai Gobi and the Dzungarian Gobi. With an area of five million hectares (19,300 square miles), this is now the

tion in the cities, as well as from mismanagement by politicians, making them realize that the allegedly so indispensable commodities of civilization were by no means a satisfactory alternative to freedom and independence. In the confined spaces of the cities, the desire for open spaces and mobility grew, and many families returned to their

third-largest natural protected region in the world.

Also, in many parts of the desert steppe, irrigation and reforestation are being promoted. New living space is to be provided for the nomads, and improvements in the quality of life are to be undertaken while still retaining the ecological balance. That is, to be sure, no easy task. For while some groups want to preserve the unique ecosystem of the desert wilderness for the future, lobbyists for mineral extraction are resisting the sealing up of the ground. To unite both nature conservation and commercial interests will be difficult. For this reason, many nomads invoke what is written in "The Secret History of the Mongols" – "Heaven and earth will strengthen our powers."

Grasslands and river landscape in the Gobi-Altai Mountains.

Prehistoric Man in the Gobi

The desert called Gobi is one of the most ancient areas of human habitation. The excavation of prehistoric finds has proved that the story of Homo sapiens began here in the Old Stone Age, the Paleolithic; for example, those from near the town of Sainshand on the route of the Trans-Mongolian Railway that connects Ulaanbaatar with Moscow and Beijing – as well as those from Mandalgobi, about 300 kilometers (188 miles) west of Sainshand. In 1969, the Russian archeologist, Aleksey P. Okladnikov (1908 to 1981), discovered tools typical of prehistoric man there, as well as hand axes of the classic Acheulean type of oval and triangular form, like those that had also been unearthed in France. These finds have now proved that people using "European hand-axe techniques" had reached Central Asia more than 230,000 years ago.

Furthermore, besides Indo-Germanic peoples, the nomadic Turkic peoples are also known to have been among the earliest inhabitants of the Gobi, although they arrived in this region at a much later date. They benefited from the favorable geological conditions of the Gobi at that time, as it did not only have ranges of sand dunes and gravel plains, but also wide grasslands, sparse vegetation, lake districts and ground water.

According to long-standing tradition, when constructing a yurt the Mongols also use felt mats that are spread on the expanding wooden frame as their main protection from the cold. Many families still make their own felt: the shorn sheep's wool is spread out loosely on a firm mat, sprinkled with boiling water and rolled up with the mat. Then the long roll is pressed by hand or drawn across the steppe with rope, causing the fibers become matted and form felt, so that a thick woolen carpet is produced.

course (…) would also have taken wings. (…) This storm was without doubt the most violent that we had yet had. (…) It was as if we were besieged and frozen in. Not only sand and dust beat against my tent, but a continuous barrage of fine gravel hammered on the felt walls. On the windward side, the yurt threatened to collapse and one roof pole after another fell down. (…) Outside, there was not a soul to be seen anywhere. Everyone, even the weather-resistant Mongols were staying safely inside."

This and similar baneful manifestations of nature are the stuff of innumerable legends in the Gobi and its surroundings, in which reality and fantasy are irretrievably confounded. In historical travel narrations, there are all manner of terrifying figures, kobolds and evil spirits. Even the Venetian explorer, Marco Polo (1254–1324) tells in his book "The Million" (The Travels of Marco Polo) of all the terrors of the great Central Asian desert:

"We can testify to the following: while riding through the desert at night, it may happen that one person remains a little behind, separating himself from his companions in order to sleep or for some other reason. When he then attempts to rejoin his fellow-travelers, he hears spirit voices that speak to him as if they were his companions, for they often call him by his name. Sometimes they lead him so far astray that he never finds the caravan again. In this way, many have found their death and have vanished without trace. We must add that even in the daytime people hear voices of spirits and frequently think they can hear various musical instruments, especially drums.

Now you know what it means to cross this desert and how arduous this is."

Furthermore, the extreme temperatures in the Gobi, which at ground level can fluctuate by up to 80° Celsius (144° Fahrenheit) have always forced the extended families of the nomads into their transportable yurts, round white felt tents in which they freeze at temperatures of up to minus 40°C (-40°F) in winter and perspire at over 30°C (86°F) of heat in summer. All of this makes it a land of extremes that condemns every living thing to harshness and austerity.

Thus, only survival artists can exist in this inhospitable area, such as the two-humped wild camel and the red-brown Onager (Asian half-ass), the light-footed saiga antelope (a member of the Bovid family), the fleet Persian goitered gazelle, the wild goat and the rare Gobi bear (masaalai), which inhabits the southwestern region of the Gobi-Altai Mountains. In addition we should mention mosquitoes, ants, spiders, bedbugs, scorpions, agile lizards and poisonous vipers. The flora of the Gobi is equally unfriendly

*Full moon over the mountains of
the Gobi-Altai where the sheep
roam (below).– A small Mongol
settlement at the foot of the Gobi-
Altai with the magical-mystical
light of the evening sun illumi-
nating their archaic slopes.
(right-hand page).*

sion area, huge rock masses were piled up to form enormously high mountains: the Himalayas were created, the highest mountains in the world, at the same time forming a barrier that was conducive to the development of desert conditions, as the height of the mountains prevented the access of rain. What had to happen did happen: while the rain clouds unloaded all their moisture on one side of the mountain walls, the other side dried out, as it lay in the precipitation shadow.

Even when tropical cyclones occasionally penetrate as far as the completely arid zones of the Gobi, they can scarcely bring moisture to the arid desert floor. Layers of hot air immediately above ground level ensure that the raindrops evaporate before they even reach their goal. These "ghost rains" are a typical phenomenon in many deserts.

The Dinosaurs' Cemetery

During the times when the present-day Gobi still had a tropical climate, there were not only numerous varieties of fish, crocodiles and turtles living among lush vegetation, but also various kinds of dinosaurs. The proof of this was found in the fall of 1923 by the team of the "Asiatic Expedition" of the American Museum of Natural History, led by Roy Chapman Andrews. The scientists had started out from Beijing on camels and had traveled to the farthest western corner of Mongolia, searching for ancient mammals and for the "Cradle of Humanity." What the expedition then found was a "paleontological garden" with more than one hundred skeletons of the genus Protoceratops (early horned dinosaurs). They lived in the Upper Cretaceous period and were up to two meters (6 feet 6 inches) tall.

They also found several clutches of fossilized dinosaur eggs that were more than 70 million years old, and in one of the cylindrical-elliptical chalk-shelled eggs, measuring up to twenty centimeters (7.8 inches), they even found the skeletal remains of a dinosaur embryo – a sensation in research into primeval times.

and consists mostly of gnarled and bristly plants. The saxaul is the most common plant of this sparse vegetation. Its bush-like, dry branches provide the nomads with excellent fuel.

How the Gobi was Formed

The deeper into the Gobi desert the traveler penetrates, the more intense is the rapid succession of visual impressions. The dimensions and expanse of this wilderness are beyond our previous experience, so that we must inevitably wonder if this immense space also has a history that is worth telling.

The answer to this question is ever-present: the surface picture of the Gobi resembles a geological diary that, with the help of methods used in the earth sciences, gives us some insight into its complex history. Here, in one of the most inhospitable regions of the world, oceans and swamps existed millions of years ago, until a geological event of stupendous proportions changed everything: the landmass of India, which at that time was isolated, a small continent, rather like Australia today, was pushed up against China so that the two continents collided. In the colli-

Since the 1920s there has been a whole series of further expeditions to the Central Gobi. Of twelve known genera of dinosaur, fossils of eight kinds have now been discovered there, giving us insight into life 65 to 248 million years ago. In particular, since the excavation of the unique "dinosaur cemetery" in the valley basin of Ukhaa Tolgod, where, in 1993, American and Mongolian scientists discovered mammals and saurians that were millions of years old and had once been buried by severe sandstorms, the Central Gobi – alongside North America – has become one of the best-known sources of dinosaur fossils.

The sand dunes of the Gobi Desert resemble the pattern of waves on the surface of an ocean.

Adventurers and Art Thieves

Europeans Explore the Gobi

Louis or merely as simple merchants, arrived in the Gobi, a true "terra incognita" or unexplored land. Motivated by curiosity, a spirit of adventure, or piety, they explored the remotest corners of Asia; the Gobi was often the focus of expeditions for geographical research.

Among the earliest European travelers who, having endured unimaginable difficulties and great dangers, arrived in the most deserted regions of Mongolia and China were, above all, Giovanni de Plano Carpini, William of Rubruck, Odoric of Pordenone, Laurentius of Portugal, Benedict of Poland, Peter of Lucalongo, Nicholas of Pistoia, Peregrinus of Castello, Arnold of Cologne, Giovanni de' Marignolli, and Bento de Gois, as well as the great Muslim scholar, Ibn Battuta.

With boldness and endurance, they all penetrated far into a foreign world full of myths and legends. And all had to contend with heat and cold, hunger and thirst, in order to become acquainted with the uniqueness of the Gobi and its inhabitants. As did the Venetian explorer, Marco Polo, who related his legendary experi-

1 Sven Hedin (1865–1952), the Swedish explorer of Asia, wearing the garments of a Mongol pilgrim. 2 The German geographer, Baron Ferdinand von Richthofen (1833–1905), journeyed through large parts of Asia.

In spite of the "horror vacuii" – the terror of the void, from the 13th century onwards many Europeans traveled to the deserts of Asia. One cannot but admire these travelers who, at the command of the Pope, as an envoy of Saint

ences to the writer Rustichello from Pisa while imprisoned in Genoa in the years 1298–99. In his book "The Million" or "The Travels of Marco Polo," he sketches an incredible picture of China and

the Mongol Empire of that period and also tells of the Lop Desert, a part of the Gobi: "To cross the desert in its entire length would, so one is told, take one year. At the narrowest point, one requires a month. Everywhere there are mountains, sand and valleys. Nothing edible (…). But I can tell you this, after one day and one night one finds drinking water, not always enough for the very large caravans, but sufficient for fifty to one hundred people with their animals. Throughout the whole desert there are waterholes separated by a day and a night's journey. You must know that three or four are brackish, but the others

are good and number in all about twenty eight."

Treasure Hunters in the Gobi
Equally dangerous expeditions to places in the Gobi that were as yet unnamed, also took place in the last quarter of the 19th century. Hoping for spectacular discoveries from their excavations, many explorers were enticed into this secretive, distant land. The Gobi was transformed into a paradise for archeologists.

Baron Ferdinand von Richthofen (1833–1905) from Germany, Sven Hedin (1865–1952) from Sweden, and Gabriel-Pierre Bonvalot (1853–1933) from France, were the first Europeans to cross large

parts of the Gobi Desert. Not forgetting Nikolai Przewalski (1839–1888), Mikhail V. Pevtsov (1843–1920) and Colonel Pyotr Kusmich Kozlov (1863–1935) from Russia; the latter discovered the remains of Khara Khoto during one of his expeditions – the lost capital of the Western Xia (Tanguts). With this sensational find, P.K. Kozlov triggered a regular international hunt for the hidden cultural treasures of the Gobi. Within a very short time, scientists of doubtful integrity from many countries traveled to the largest desert in Asia to drag back with them tonnes of frescoes, sculptures, and ancient manu-

3 Sven Hedin with the participants in his expedition of 1927/28, which led him though the Gobi Desert and into Chinese Turkestan.

scripts from forgotten temples and monasteries. Many of these "art thieves" justified their actions, saying they wanted to preserve the treasures of the Gobi for coming generations. But in the nightly bombing raids on London and Berlin during the Second World War, more art treasures from the Gobi were destroyed than plundering, earthquakes or new irrigation systems could ever have resulted in.

Where the Son of the Blue Wolf Rests

With Camels and on Foot through the Deserts of Inner Mongolia

"I am no hermit, but, strangely, it is this lonely region that truly fascinates me, so that sometimes I climb a mountain away from the camp and gaze for hours at the valleys and across the land, as if in a dream. This dead, grey landscape that is only broken up by scattered green patches and that is otherwise without tree or bush impresses me again and again by its solitude and vast distances."

Paul Lieberenz, *With Sven Hedin Across the Deserts of Asia*

Beneath the wide arch of the Milky Way, I was trying to take shelter behind the crumbling wall of a house. Danger threatened in the form of a police patrol that had jumped out of a jeep some twenty meters away. Shouldering their weapons, they stormed

Achill Moser loads up his camels, which patiently carry heavy loads, for his long march through the Gobi Desert. – He very seldom sees rivers carrying water in the wilderness. – Walking through the ocean of sand in the Gobi, along narrow ridges (right-hand page).

into the public cook-shop where I had been offered a place to stay for the night. Just in time, Tsong, a young Chinese man, was able to warn me about the patrol that wanted to arrest me for questioning. Someone suspected me of being a spy or a smuggler. What nonsense!

After almost four weeks in the virtually endless expanses of the Gobi Desert, with two camels carrying all my belongings, above all, drinking water, food and a storm tent, I had arrived at the village of Minqin. Here I rested for a few days and took leave of my camels, in order to continue my journey in the desert on foot.

That is how I came to be sitting at a table with some local people in the little cook-shop, eating an evening meal, when a young policeman wanted to check my papers. He skeptically examined my official permit for a desert hike in the Gobi. Finally he made it clear to me that I should have reported to him. Incensed, he wanted to confiscate my passport. I refused. There

was an argument. As he left angrily, he ordered me to come to the police station the next morning. Harassment pure and simple.

Shortly afterwards, Tsong, a young student from Beijing who was here in the north of China on a visit to his grandparents, told me that some soldiers wanted to take me away for interrogation the same evening. He had heard this purely by chance. Lucky for me. I now had enough time to get away before the police patrol arrived.

Under cover of darkness, Tsong now led me out of Minqin and then went a long way around the village to return unnoticed to the house of his relatives. I continued on my way alone. Out into the desert, into Inner Mongolia. Covering an area of almost 1.2 million square kilometers (463,200 square miles), it is the third-largest province of China – with the status of an autonomous region. One half is desert, the other half, pastureland. Nineteen million people live here, of whom 16 million are Han Chinese. Besides the Hui and Manchurians, the 2.5 million Mongolians are the most important minority group.

Following the Traces of a Forgotten People

My aim was to travel on foot through the former realm of the Western Xia people, a group related to the Tibetans who originally came from the region of Qinghai Lake (Koko Nor), in the north-eastern section of the Tibetan Plateau. Between 1032 and 1227, the Western Xia (also known as Tanguts) ruled the area covering Inner Mongolia, as well as northern China along the Silk Road and into the province of Gansu.

The Western Xia (or Hsi Hsia) are a legendary people who developed a unique form of writing. It was first discovered in the caves of Dunhuang at the beginning of the 20th century, and which the experts have still not fully deciphered. After ruling for 200 years, the Western Xia were attacked by the Mongols in the year 1227. At that time, the Western Xia had acknowledged Genghis Khan's dominance in Central Asia, but they did not support the Mongol troops against China. This led to a war in which the hordes of Mongol riders wiped out the Western Xia with fire and sword.

Where the empire of the Western Xia was once situated, there are now only wide expanses of desert: mainly the Gobi and its environs, which include the deserts of Badain Jaran, the Tengger and the Ordos. All these are expanses as large as oceans, and I wanted to cross them from west to east, from the famous temple caves at Dunhuang – considered one of the most precious repositories of Buddhism and once part of the Western Xia Empire – to Ejen Khoro, a shrine to Genghis Khan, whose death is closely connected to the fall of the Western Xia. The distance I planned to cover totaled about 1,400 kilometers (875 miles).

Months of planning lay behind me when I flew to Beijing (Peking), equipped with a small vocabulary of Chinese words. From the capital city, I flew to Urumqi in Sinkiang, the largest

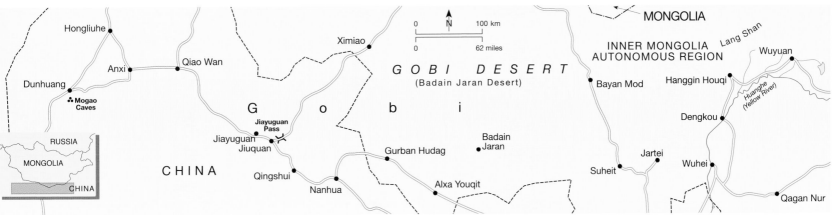

province in China. From there I traveled by truck to Dunhuang at the edge of the Gobi desert, an oasis surrounded by aspen, elm and ash trees.

Fifteen kilometers (9 miles) southeast of this former caravan center, between rugged mountains and sand dunes, lie the splendid temple caves of Dunhuang (also called the Mogao Grottoes). This monastic complex was once a center of devotion and thanksgiving. The caravan guides prayed here and sought protection from the gods before setting out along the Silk Road to travel around the dangerous desert regions of western China.

Crossing the cemetery of the old Buddhist community, I reached two newly erected gates of honor. Beyond these, the main temple rises at the cliff wall. On both sides of it there is a steep cliff face, 1,600 meters (21,250 feet) long and honeycombed with numerous small caves. Of the original 1,000 caves, 492 have been preserved. They contain the unique treasures of Mogao.

Between the fourth and the fourteenth century, during heyday of the Silk Road, Buddhist monks chiseled a five-story cave settlement into the rock wall here and painted frescoes that today still cover a surface area of 45,000 square meters (53,550 square yards).

At the bazaars in the oases, Mongols, Tajiks, Chinese, and Uyghurs barter for goods and the noodlemakers go about their daily handiwork. Not far from the monastic temple of Dunhuang, there are dense groves of trees in the wadi of the former Dachuan River (left-hand page).

The massive entrance gate of the monastic complex in Dunhuang (above) leads to the Mogao Caves where holy stupas of the Buddhists stand as eternal guardians of the faith (top).

The main theme of the cave paintings is Buddha who, during the late Han Dynasty (25–220 AD), traveled to China from Gandara in present-day Pakistan, passing through Kashmir, Afghanistan and the Tarim Basin. No other place on earth grants us such comprehensive insight into one thousand years of Buddhist culture.

When the traffic on the Silk Road declined in the 14th century, the Mogao Caves were forgotten. Shifting sand dunes buried the temple complex and the monks' cells. Not until 1899 were they rediscovered by the Taoist monk Wang Yuanlu, who was searching for his religious predecessors in this region. With the help of some laborers, he dug several caves free from the sand and came across a secret chamber in which an entire library of eastern Asian knowledge was contained: Buddhist texts in various languages, wide-ranging historical material, some ceremonial equipment and testimonies to the faith of the Manicheans and Nestorians.

Altogether 50,000 documents, dating from the period between the third and eleventh centuries, were found. The dry desert climate had enabled them to survive for more than 900 years. Among them were the finds in cave no. 17, where the envoys of the Western Xia had walled in large numbers of paintings and manuscripts with details of their life and their rulers.

Archeologists have now been able to decipher more than 6,000 symbols of the writing of the Western Xia. Thus it was learnt that the Western Xia were translating classical teaching texts of Buddhism, as well as Chinese classics, as early as the 11th century.

After the discovery of the lost cultural treasures of Dunhuang, however, not even the Chinese provincial government of Gansu acknowledged their value. Some European archeologists were therefore able to purchase thousands of texts, scroll paintings and sculptures at ridiculously low prices.

Some scientists even painted the frescoes with special adhesive and then ripped the thousand-year-old paintings off the cave walls, like transfers, using a strip of gauze soaked in glue. Whole cartloads of paintings, drawings and manuscript scrolls were

See page 132

The monastic complex of Dunhuang, at the edge of the Gobi Desert, is one of the major sanctuaries of Buddhism (below). Of the 1,000 former monks' cells, 492 have been preserved and contain unique frescoes and more than 3,000 sculptures. The motifs of the brightly colored pictures mainly focus on the story of Buddha's life (left-hand page).

127

Walking through the ocean of sand of the Gobi Desert.

An All-purpose Animal

The Camel – The Gentle Rebel of the Gobi

In many regions of Mongolia, the camel is the most important means of transport. Only a few decades ago, heavily loaded caravans of camels were the only way to bring goods to certain, remote areas. Bearing a load of around 250 kilograms, a camel can cover more than 40 kilometers (25 miles) in one day. A camel can also go without water for up to two weeks while traveling, until it is able to drink the precious liquid at a river or well.

The camel is a member of the order of cloven-hoofed animals (Artiodactyla) and the suborder Tylopoda (meaning: padded foot). It is a most undemanding animal, a long-legged pass-climber and ruminant with several stomach chambers. Its adaptability to extreme surroundings make it a "water-saver" in the truest sense. We must distinguish between the two varieties of camel: one is the one-humped Dromedary (camelus dromedarius) that lives primarily in North Africa and Arabia. It can do without water for up to two weeks, losing up to 30 percent of its body weight in that time. But it can also absorb water extremely fast; up to 100 liters (26 gallons) in 10 minutes.

On the contrary, the two-humped Bactrian camel is at home mainly in the arid regions of Central Asia. A small group also inhabits areas of the Gobi Desert. These wild camels are the ancestors of the so-called "domesticated camel" that is used mainly in Asia as a pack animal and for riding and also as a supplier of meat, milk and dung. The latter is used by the nomads as fuel for their fires.

4

5

In Mongolia, where the nomads still mainly live from camel breeding, the Mongolian Camel, a member of the species "camelus bactrianus" is found. Almost 65 percent of the entire camel population is concentrated in the former empire of Genghis Khan in the steppes and deserts of the Gobi.

Above all, in the mountainous regions, as well as in areas where roads and trails are in poor condition, the camel is still the only means of transport. Furthermore, the Mongolian nomads use camel milk as a drink and for making other milk products. Even camel meat is highly prized as excellent fare, alongside beef. But the most important product of the Mongolian camel is its wool. Each year about five to seven kilograms (11-15 pounds) of wool can be won from one animal.

There is probably no other animal that permits itself to be used in so many ways as the camel. For more than one thousand years, Mongolian camels have been bearing loads of up to six hundredweight (300 kilograms) through the loneliest regions in the world. When they occasionally have a wound caused by the constant chafing of the load, the blisters are burnt away with a hot iron. Then the nomads rub the wound with sand, load up the animal again and continue their journey through blistering hot deserts as or across icy steppes. Without the camel, people could not survive in the most extreme environments in the world. It is the ideal animal for the desert: its eyes have large eyelashes and strong tear production that prevent sand getting into the eyes in a sandstorm; the nostrils are narrow slits that can be closed by activating a muscle, when the wind is fierce; the divided and fleshy upper lip enables it to tear off thorny twigs; the vast quantity of saliva produced in the mouth protects it from injuries when crushing up gnarled bushes.

Moreover, when a camel absorbs large quantities of water, its red blood cells can increase to two hundred times their normal volume. And finally, in extreme heat, a thirsty camel can raise its body temperature to 42° Celsius (197.6° Fahrenheit) and prevent further loss of fluid through a controlled "fever".

131

finally brought by the caravans to Europe, where the majority of these treasures were destroyed in the air raids on London and Berlin during the Second World War.

Keeping in Step with Your Soul

I left the Mogao Caves in early March and headed into the desert. A livestock trader had loaned me two camels for four weeks. During that time, I wanted to reach Minqin at the edge of the Tengger Desert. From there the camels would be transported back by truck.

I had spent one week before my departure becoming acquainted with the camels. I have had many years of experience with the "ships of the desert" in Asia and Africa: I have traveled through 25 of the world's deserts on more than 30 expeditions, lasting a total of five years. All of these were on foot or by camel "at a speed that the soul can keep in step with." Keeping to this principle, I follow, like a nomad, the forgotten caravan trails and routes of historical explorers, which – over periods of weeks or

months – lead me to legendary ruined cities, mysterious monasteries and magnificent caves full of paintings, many of which had been thought lost for centuries.

During the first few days I made rapid progress. Trying to find the right rhythm, I kept pace with the swaying camels through wonderful landscapes in which wide fields of sand alternated with scree and rock fields.

The distance I covered daily was a maximum of 40 to 50 kilometers (25-31 miles); the camels patiently carried the baggage: tent, isolation mat, sleeping bag, fleece clothing, down jacket, camera equipment, stove and, of course, supplies of food. I had brought muesli, corned beef, beans, tomatoes, onions, milk powder, glucose and fruit. One third of the load was fodder for the animals, and plenty of water. Nonetheless, I knew I would have to rely on the scattered villages and waterholes.

I also had maps and a compass for precise orientation. If I should have any doubts about my orientation, I should still be able to find my position by the stars, as I had learned to do from the Tuareg in the Sahara many years ago.

Occasionally the ruins of defensive ramparts, of gates and buildings loom up out of the sand in the Gobi; the remains of former oases that were often lost in the sea of the desert for centuries.

Ruined City in the Desert

When I entered one of the remote villages that lay along my route, I was immediately surrounded by a crowd of friendly people. Curious men and women often pushed so close that I worried that the camels might kick out at them blindly in self-defense. At some point, I therefore decided to visit the villages without the camels. Before I went to buy water and other supplies; I would leave the animals and my baggage outside the village.

Beyond Choushuidun, I turned south and arrived at the Hei River as it wound towards the north. The Mongols call it "Etsin Gol," and its water once guaranteed the existence of the desert city of Khara Khoto. Some years before, I had followed this river bed with a car as far as the Chinese-Mongolian border. It was an adventurous journey that had brought me to a ruined city in the ocean of sand.

I will never forget how I suddenly saw the ruins of defensive walls, of gates and buildings looming up in the desert: the "Black City" of Khara Khoto.

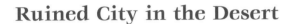

Rock Drawings in Ancient Mongolia

Wherever smooth stone surfaces are found in the remote mountainous regions of Mongolia, one also finds rock drawings from the Bronze Age. Many of them were places of sacrifice in ancient times, shrines under the open sky, or they reflected the life of early hunters and livestock herders. Other representations, such as those on the banks of the Chuluut River in northern Mongolia, depicted the universe; in particular, the pictures of bulls take on special meaning when one remembers the prominence they once had in the cosmic ideas of primitive people. At Mankhan (not far from the Altai Mountains, in the Three River Valley Ishgin Tolgoy) there are more than 150 rock drawings of antelope, bisons, elks, deer, camels, horses, and snakes that are equally wonderful.

Not far away are the rock drawings in the Khoit Tzenkher caves, where people of the Late Stone Age painted wild sheep, ibex, cows, bulls, snakes, and suns – as well as a two-humped Bactrian camel, which is considered the oldest drawing of a camel in the world. Not forgetting the depictions of mammoths and ostriches that existed about 15,000 years ago in ancient Mongolia.

The Swedish explorer Sven Hedin and his camera man Paul Lieberenz had been here in the 1920s. In his book "With Sven Hedin Across the Deserts of Asia," Lieberenz described the re-discovery of the legendary lost city of Khara Khoto: "Slowly we approached the city that had only been found two decades previously, re-discovered by the Russian, Kozlov, who came across it in 1909. Old descriptions tell of this former metropolis; without doubt it is the city of Etsina that Marco Polo describes as lying 'at the beginning of the sand desert in the province of Tangut,' but its location was unknown for many centuries."

At the markets in the oases you can haggle for everything from an apple to a finely-carved piece of furniture (above).

At the Huang-he (Yellow River), Mongols and Chinese build large transport rafts from inflated pigskins (right).

In the year 1227, the cavalry of Genghis Khan invaded Khara Khoto and razed to the ground the capital of the Western Xia, which was surrounded by a 500-meter-long city wall. In August of the same year, the founder of the Mongol Empire and conqueror, Genghis Khan, died. Whether this occurred in battle against the Western Xia or some weeks later as a result of a fall from his horse is a mystery that will probably never be solved.

Equally shrouded in legend is the question of whether there were survivors of the Western Xia after the battle for Khara Khoto.

Scientists have now deciphered documents from the Ming period (14th to 17th century) that point to the existence of the former Western Xia after the battle against the Mongol army. According to these sources, there are people living today in the mountainous northwestern region of the Chinese province Sichuan who speak a language that demonstrates many similarities to that of the Western Xia. But there is no final proof. The

place of refuge that the Western Xia may found is still hidden in the secret darkness of which legends are made.

Where the Spirits of the Dead Appear at Night

More than 150 years after the storming of the fortress of Khara Khoto and the destruction of the Western Xia, the reign of the Mongol king Khara Bator over his people in Asia happened right here. He was entrenched with his people behind the walls of the reconstructed fortress of Khara Khoto, while the superior armies of the Chinese Ming Dynasty were massed in front of the walls. But instead of storming the fortress, the Chinese diverted the river Etsin Gol (Black River), the only source of water for Khara Khoto. They surrounded the desert city and laid siege to it.

When the Mongol king realized the hopelessness of the situation, he killed his family and then took his own life with his sword. His soldiers still fought on, but they were soon slaughtered by the Ming, who left the corpses behind, unburied, in the destroyed garrison. According to legend, the spirits of the dead still wander here at night.

From Gaotai, not far from the Longshou Range (3,616 meters/11,860 feet), I take course towards the Badain Jaran Desert. With an area of 47,000 square kilometers (18,142 square miles), it is the third-largest desert in China and adjoins the Gobi. Eighty percent of the Badain Jaran Desert consists of shifting sand dunes, some of which reach a height of 300 meters (984 feet). Also, here in western Inner Mongolia, small inland lakes often create small pockets of fertile land. Their water is usually salty, but at the shore or between these lakes, fresh drinking water bubbles up. Nomads water their herds at these places and fill their water bags.

Sandstorm

On Day Seventeen, leaden-colored skies covered the desert. Wild whistling sounds filled the air. The wind suddenly seemed to come from all sides. The ground swayed and the compass needle spun like a top. And everything around me disappeared into a grey fog. Without needing a command, the camels knelt down, turned their heads away from the wind and their backs towards the whirling sand. I moistened their chaps with some tumblers of water, tied a wet cloth over my face and pressed in close to the animals.

Like ocean breakers, waves of sand as high as a house lashed over us. Everywhere there was whining and screaming – a symphony of terror. I was forced to remain in my shelter for three hours. Then the storm abated and the sand masses became still again.

The Desert Demands Total Affection or Total Rejection

After 26 days, I took leave of my camels in Minqin, where I escaped a police patrol just in time. Now the second stage of my desert journey began: on foot, with only a backpack, I wanted to experience the desert at first hand. I reveled in this direct contact with the desert and again and again I was astonished by the splendor of the landscapes and the sensations alternating between fascination and fear.

Maybe only someone who loves the desert can feel this way. For me, at least, the deserts are the regions of the world that demand total affection or total rejection. One may love the desert, or leave it as quickly as possible, but one must decide.

In the Land of the Spirits

Equipped only with a backpack containing the most necessary items and twelve liters (3.2 gallons) of water, I set out on foot – without camels – towards Hongliuyuan and Dongzhen. In front of me lay the wavy, sandy ocean of the Tengger Desert. The name refers to "spirits" in the Mongolian language.

With an area of 36,000 square kilometers (13,896 square miles), the Tengger forms part of the Alashan Desert, as well as

The faces of many Mongolian women have been sculpted by their nomadic life, exposed to the wind, sun and cold (left).
In the Gobi Desert, where the grass steppe merges into sand desert, the camels of the nomads have lots of freedom to roam and, when needed, are driven to the yurt (right-hand page).

of the Gobi. Immediately after the revolution of 1949, the Chinese attempted to get the enormous movements of the sands of the Tengger under control. Barriers were erected along a distance of 140 kilometers (88 miles), and a railway line built, but it remains a difficult task to keep the tracks clear. Violent sandstorms can occur at any season, causing huge drifts of sand and preventing normal rail traffic.

My hike through the Tengger was anything but easy. Sometimes I felt as if I was making no progress at all toward reaching my goals. In particular, taking bearings with a compass proved extremely difficult in the undulating, sandy terrain. The points from which I took my bearings were often up to fifty kilometers (31 miles) distant. If I failed to not concentrate completely, errors occured in the compass traverse. These were the moments when I desperately needed a sense of achievement. For example, the discovery of a far away point in the seeming void. A confirmation of my accurate navigation work. A huge uplift for the soul.

After six days in the Tengger Desert, I arrived at the town of Alxa Zuoqi, an oasis in a vast sea of sand. Soon I would reach the Helan Mountains, once revered by the Western Xia people as a holy place. Here they entombed nine of their kings and more than seventy of their leading statesmen. The mausoleums are spread over an area measuring four by ten kilometers (2.5 x 6 miles); the

stone altars, twenty meters (66 feet) high, resembled small pyramids. In spite of weathering, their seven-layered, octagonal shape can still be easily recognized.

To the Memorial to Genghis Khan

After several days' march, I came to the Yellow River, the Huangho, where a ferryman took me across on a junk. Farther and farther, my way led me in a northeasterly direction. I had now reached the Ordos Desert, enclosed by a huge bend of the Yellow River. It is an impressive wilderness region with plenty of groundwater that ensures strong plant growth. Swamps and river valleys alternate with terraced land and grassy hills. These are followed by large, flat areas of quicksand and high ranges of sand dunes.

It was already the beginning of May when I lost my way between Narin Nur and Juntuliang. I made more and more navigational errors. My internal batteries were empty. I mobilized my last reserves of strength, worked constantly with the compass and map, and drifted around hour by hour. Four times I inwardly gave up. Only the desire to reach my goal drove me on.

Then I met some camel herders, and found out where I was. In their yurt they gave me hot tea, bread, boiled mutton and yoghurt. For weeks I had not been so pampered.

And then, on day 61 of my desert journey, I arrived at the town of Ejen Khoro in the Ordos region. I had lost more than seven kilograms (15 pounds) in weight. But I was in high spirits. In front of me I saw the lush green of the shrine and memorial to Genghis Khan erected by the Chinese. His bones do not lie here – scientific research has now proved that. But in spirit, this memorial is intended to unite the people of Inner and Outer Mongolia. It is a place with powerful political and cultural symbolism. Eight white palace tents like those that Genghis Khan once lived in are accommodated here in three octagonal buildings with yurt-like domed roofs. Their glazed tiles shone in the sunshine. Right into the 1870s, a sarcophagus with relics and the remains of Genghis Khan is said to have stood here, until it was burned by Chinese Moslems.

Passing several men in blue robes and yellow sashes who, as descendants of the Mongol guards, watch over the shrine, I entered the mausoleum where, as expected, I saw the statue of the Mongol prince, carved in stone. On an altar, candles had been lit and flowers placed beside them.

To the annoyance of the Chinese government, the people here in the curve of the Ordos still revere Genghis Khan and bring him sacrificial offerings. To the people of Inner Mongolia, he is

still the son of the legendary blue wolf that, at the desire of the Almighty, took a white doe as a wife. Young Mongols still tell this tale today in their yurts.

As I left the memorial, a group of Mongolian riders with shaggy horses and heavily laden camels moved northwards: a little caravan, passing through the pale green distance. A breathtaking expanse – mysterious, unconfined, timeless, as the nomads need it to be, so that they can live.

Magnificent range of sand dunes in the Gobi Desert.

The Mongolians' Favorite Sport

The Nadaam Festival

At the annual Nadaam Festival, the best archers (1), horse riders (5) and wrestlers (6) compete. Naturally, not only men ride horses, but the women are also keen riders, so that statistically there are still ten horses for every Mongolian

In Ulan Bator, the traditional Nadaam Festival begins with a large funfair, after which 512 wrestlers take up the challenge (in past times there were more than one thousand). They have progressed to the final through qualifying rounds that last for months. Whereas the wrestlers used to appear naked, they now wear a garment resembling swim trunks and a short jacket of red or light blue silk, so that the back and a section of the arms are covered. The toes of their boots are turned upwards, so that when fighting they do not scrape the earth open – for that is the face of Buddha.

Wrestling is, as it has always been, the favorite sport of the Mongolians. It takes place on the second day of the festival and the winners are commended by the President and receive expensive prizes. Archery, on the other hand, has been declining in significance in recent years. The number of Mongols who can use a bow and arrow has decreased. Nonetheless, there are still competitions for individuals and for teams. People like to reminisce about the Nadaam Festival of 1937, when an 80-year-old man hit the target with all 80 arrows. Just as sensational was the victory of the Mongolian liberation hero, Sükhbaatar, who held the office of Minister of War when he won the first prize at archery in 1922.

When the field of participants for the horse race is fixed, all other Nadaam activities are broken off and people congregate in the huge city of yurts at Buyant Ukhaa, eight kilometers (5 miles) outside Ulan Bator, where everyone watches the finish of the race. Before the race starts, the jockeys – girls and boys aged between 5 and 13 years in colorful costumes and wearing a cone-shaped cap – parade around the race course, singing songs.

Then the races begin in the various categories: two-year-olds run 15 kilometers (9 miles), four-year-olds 25 kilometers (16 miles), five-

way back in history and was not only held for the amusement of the people. Above all, it was an opportunity for the many warriors of the Mongol Empire to demonstrate their strength and skills.

The actual name of these competitions, which are referred to by the Mongolians as "the three sports for men" (eriyn gurwan

Mongols, which ended in the year 1758 with the destruction and mass slaughter of many Mongol tribes, the Nadaam Festival lost its significance, as the Manchu did all they could to ensure that no large gatherings of people took place in Mongolia, which might have served to strengthen the defeated nation. Only in 1921,

4

when the communist government took over and combined the Nadaam Festival with a public holiday, Day of Victory of the People's Revolution (July 11 and 12), was new life breathed into the Mongolian games.

Now, regional competitions in the three sports take place everywhere in summer, while the "National Nadaam" is held in the capital, Ulan Bator. In Inner Mongolia, the Nadaam Festival is not held until the fall, and the date of the games is determined by the lunar calendar.

5

6

year-olds 28 kilometers (18 miles), stallions 30 kilometers (19 miles), and still older horses must cover a distance of 35 kilometers (22 miles). Special honors are awarded only to the "Very First of Ten Thousand," while the young jockeys receive medals and gifts. Three traditional sports form the heart of the famous Mongolian

Nadaam Festival: wrestling, archery and horse racing. The name of the festival actually means something like "competition and fun." And in that spirit, many sportsmen test their skills against each other every year at the same time in the sports stadiums of Ulan Bator. The tradition of the Nadaam Festival goes a long

naadam), also originated in early times. A weathered memorial stone is a reminder of an ancient Nadaam festival, and the inscription on the stone tells of an archer called Esunge Mergen who once shot an arrow more than 500 meters (1,650 feet).

After the conflict between the Manchu Dynasty and the Western

The spectators stream into Ulan Bator from all over the country (2), form groups along the race course (3) or find seats in the stadium where the archers are little way off to the side, selecting their arrows for the archery competition (4).

141

With the Gobi-Altai in the background: a sand dune at Dorgon Nuur.

Planning your Journey

the territory lies at a height of more than 1,000 meters (3,280 feet). The highest point is Khuiten Uul (4,734 m/ 15,528 ft), located in the western Tavan-Bogd Massif, which forms part of the Mongolian Altai. In the northernmost region of the country, the lowest point can be found: the salt lake Khukh Nuur or "Blue Lake" (552 meters/ 1,811 ft) above sea level).

Fascinating plant life in the high mountains of the Altai.

Flora and Fauna

As a result of the low density of population, the plant and animal world of Mongolia is relatively rich and diverse. At present, 2,500 different varieties of plant are known; these occur in widely differing veg-

etation zones ranging from north to south: mountain taiga, alpine zone, mountain forest steppe, steppe, desert steppe, desert zone. Within this series of zones, a huge diversity of plant life can be found: there are tall grasses and herbs,

A transport ferry at the lake Tsagaan Nuur in northern Mongolia.

Name

The official name of the country is Mongolia (Mongol Uls); until 1990 it was still a People's Republic. The name refers to the word Mongol, which means something like "the courageous ones."

Size / Situation / Region

Mongolia is situated in the northern part of Central Asia and covers an area of 1.565 million square kilometers (604,000 square miles).

It is a vast natural region, about four times the size of the United Kingdom, or twice the size of Texas. To the north, Mongolia has a border with Russia, and to the south with China. It is a land of wide steppes, deserts, rivers, lakes, and large mountain ranges. The greatest distance from west to east is 2,400 kilometers (1,500 miles), while Mongolia stretches for 1,263 kilometers (789 miles) from north to south. The total length of the national border of Mongolia is 8,300 kilometers (5,188 miles), and 80 percent of

Magnificent bloom at Hogon Nuur.

different types of edelweiss and gentian, spruce, pine, cedar and other conifers; Siberian larch, aspen and birch trees, cranberries and bilberries, ferns and lichens; also saxaul bushes and bulbiferous and medicinal plants, of which about 400 varieties are used in traditional Mongolian medicine.

The animal world in Mongolia is equally varied: besides a wealth of fish and bird life, including eagles, hawks, vultures, mountain partridges, kites, swans, and quails, other species include the brown bear, the Altai mountain goat, mountain sheep (argali), fox, steppe polecat and tiger polecat, marmot, stone marten, snow leopard, wolverine and wolf. Other animals that inhabit Mongolia are the last existing wild camels, the wild donkey, the Asian wild horse (Przewalski's horse), the ibex, saiga antelope, the Persian goitered gazelle, the red deer, and the rare Gobi bear.

A Mongolian child in the Khangai Mountains.

A nomad skeptically examines a gift from a guest.

Population

More than 85 percent of the 2.6 million inhabitants of Mongolia are Mongols, and the majority of these are Khalkha Mongols. From ancient times, the region occupied by Mongolia has been a melting pot of peoples representing many different language groups. There is no discrimination of minorities here. The Kazakhs (about seven percent of the population) who live in the far west of the country have a special position, because of the differences in their culture, language and religion. Other minority groups are the Tsaatan, Tuva, Darkhad, Uriankhai, Dariganga, Dzakhchin, Buryat, Bayad, and Öölt.

Language

The official language is (Khalkha) Mongolian. There are also minority languages, for example, Kazakh, Tuvan and Russian; the latter is still widespread, particularly in the

north of Mongolia. English has now replaced German as the second most important foreign language.

Politics and Administration

Mongolia is a republic and, since 1992, a parliamentary democracy and constitutional state. In the year 2005 the President was Nambaryn

Enkhbayar and the Prime Minister was Tsakia Elbegdorj.

Mongolia is a centralized state, divided into 21 *aimags* (provinces), which in turn are divided into so-called *sum*, sometimes called *sumon*, each of which is divided again into several districts called *bag*.

Economy

For centuries the economic structure of Mongolia has been based on nomadic animal husbandry with a barter economy; the nomads move with their herds of cattle, goats, sheep, camels, and yaks from one area of grazing land to another. The nutritional habits of the nomadic population were adapted to the animal products from their own economy. Now, especially in the larger cities of Ulan Bator (Ulaanbaatar), Darkhan and Erdenet, there are numerous industrial plants and mining operations for fluorspar, iron

Traditional costumes of the Tuva people.

Discovering Mongolia

Four Tours Through a Wide Land

1 From the "Three Beauties" to Vulture Canyon

You can spend eventful days in the eastern part of the Gobi, 550 kilometers (344 miles) southwest of Ulan Bator. You should fly or drive to Dalandsadgad. Northwest of the town, you should find a place to stay in one of the tourist camps, so that the next day the experience of the impressive mountain range of the Gurvansaikhan ("Three Beauties"),

running from northwest to southeast, can begin. In the eastern massif, about 70 kilometers (44 miles) from Dalandsadgad (the largest oasis of the Mongolian Gobi), there are deep ravine-like canyons with imposing cliff faces. One of these canyons is called Yolin Am or Vulture Canyon – a ravine 200 meters (656 feet) deep that gets progressively narrower and through which a mountain stream races. In winter the crystal-clear water freezes right to the bottom. Even summer tem-

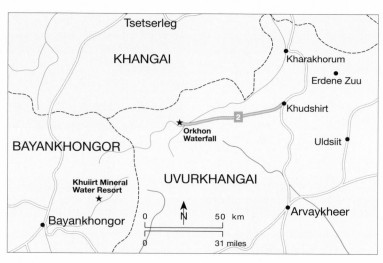

peratures cannot melt the ice completely. It is not unusual for sections of up to 200–300 meters (656-984 feet) to remain frozen. On rocky projections from the cliff and ridge-like crests of this canyon, carrion-eating vultures and other rare birds of prey have their habitat, as well as argali sheep and mountain goats.

At the entrance to Vulture Canyon, the animal museum with dinosaurs made of papier mache and stuffed snow leopards is worth a visit.

2 From the medicinal springs at Khujirt to the Orkhon waterfall

At the eastern borders of the East Khangai Mountains, 300 kilometers (188 miles) southwest of Ulan Bator, lies Khujirt, one of the oldest thermal spas in Mongolia, where water from the many hot springs

has for decades been used successfully to heal various illnesses: circulation problems, digestive problems, nervous complaints and heart disease, joint and limb pain and respiratory infections. As early as the 1940s, a sanatorium complex was built in Khujirt, with a bath house fed by healing hot spring waters that contain, among other things, chlorine, germanium, potassium, sodium, sulfates and uranium. Khujirt is also an excellent starting point for a trip to the marvelous Orkhon waterfall (65 kilometers/ 41 miles from Khujirt) where the waters of the Ulaan Gol plunge 20 meters (66 feet) in a wide cascade and with a load roaring noise into the Orkhon River – a paradise for hobby anglers. Below the falls, the waters of the Orkhon flow through a basalt gorge of more than 130 meters (426 feet) in width, where the

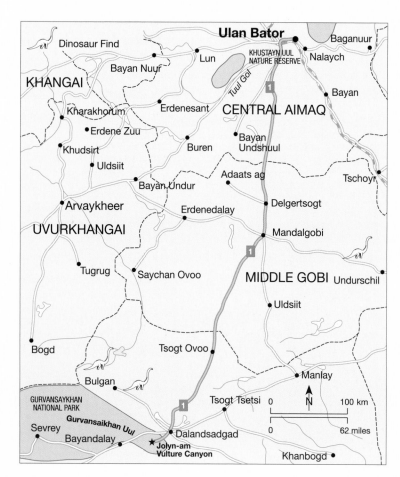

ROUTE OVERVIEW
Route 1
Route 2
Route 3
Route 4

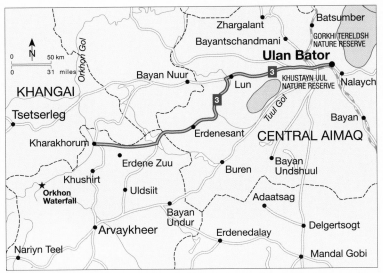

actly what Kharakhorum looked like. Until now, individual excavations have only uncovered what was once the floor of the palace, with the base of a missing column, and a majestic street that separated the Chinese quarter from the Moslem quarter. Outside of the former city walls of Kharakhorum, there are three stone tortoises which according to Mongolian symbolism represent great wisdom and longevity.

4 Excursion to the Gobi: To the giant saurians and trees of stone

The best place to begin a desert tour in the Gobi is the oasis of Dalandsadgad. Traveling by jeep, the journey leads westwards to "Dinosaur Land" at Bayanzag (as well as to the Nemeget Basin), where significant finds of dinosaur remains were discovered between the pink sandstone cliffs. In an area of sand dunes 100 kilometers (63 miles) long, called Gurvan Tesgiyn Hooloy by the Mongolians, numerous graves with fossilized dinosaur

bones have been found. Other discoveries around the old saxaul forest of Bayanzag include complete nests containing dinosaur eggs and their shells from the Cretaceous period. These fossils had lain in the ground, undiscovered, for more than 70 million years. (Some of the most interesting dinosaur finds can also be seen in the dinosaur rooms of the Museum of Natural History in Ulan Bator.)

A journey from Dalandsadgad in an easterly direction (via Manlay, Mandakh, Sainshand, and Khuvsgul to Khatanbulag) provides an equally fascinating view of the geological "diary" of Mongolia. Around 100 kilometers (63 miles) northwest of Khatanbulag, is the "stone forest of Suihent" – a bizarre region with petrified trees that are estimated to be 100 million years old. These fossil trees, up to 20 meters (66 feet) tall and with a diameter of up to 1.5 meters (5 feet), cover an area of approximately 500 by 80 meters (547 x 87 yards). They are proof that a warm and humid climate once prevailed in the region of Mongolia.

basin-shaped valley floor is covered in huge larch trees.

3 Kharakhorum – where the past is alive

The lost city of Kharakhorum, once the splendid capital of the legendary Mongol emperors, is still worth visiting, even though much imagination is required to visualize how this royal seat, described by the Venetian explorer Marco Polo and the Franciscan monk William of Rubruck, might have looked in the 13th century. A large part of this Mongol metropolis, which was founded in 1220, is now hidden un-

der the earth and overgrown with thick steppe grass. Although archeologists have now made numerous discoveries, we still do not know ex-

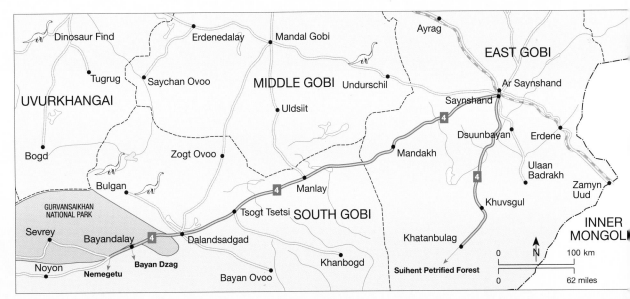

ore, gold, copper, molybdenum, phosphates, wolfram, zinc and tin. Besides light industries and food production, there are the beginnings of a petro-chemical industry. Many former state-owned enterprises were privatized after the new political orientation. Only the main foreign currency earners, mining and the production of cashmere, are still run by the state. Permanent budgetary deficits, foreign debts, loss of purchasing power and the lack of alternatives to nomadic animal husbandry will

Religion

Tibetan Buddhism, which has been the influential and primary faith of the nomads and the population of the steppe since the 16th century, is still the most common religion in Mongolia. Shamanism and nature worship, as well as Christian influences, exist as well. The Kazakhs are Moslems. Since 1991, the Dalai Lama, who is regarded as their spiritual leader by the Mongolians, has visited Mongolia several times, to en-

Best Time to Travel

The best time to travel is during the months from June to September. In July and August however, one must expect heavy summer rain showers. It can rain a great deal, especially in the north. In the steppe and desert regions of the Gobi, on the other hand, it can be

An ovoo in the Khangai Mountains: the domicile of local deities and spirits.

Modern styling: Ulan Bator at night.

A lesson at a private school.

Layover on a domestic flight.

continue to cause problems for the people of Mongolia for a long time to come.

courage the believers and to dedicate temples and preside over religious ceremonies.

As Long as there is Meat and Milk...

Boodog, Boorsog and Airag – Food and Drink in the Steppe

Preparing food is a task that keeps mainly the wives and daughters busy all day long. While aaruul (curd cheese) is drying on the roof of a yurt, inside the tent little pockets of flour are deep-fried in fat, baked noodles are stirred into the meat – a favorite meal in Mongolia – and noodles are made.

Since times long past, the Mongols have believed that dishes containing meat are essential for good health. So, today, meat and milk products still form the basis of their diet. Meat is usually boiled or eaten half-raw. In this way trace elements that raise the nutritional value remain in the blood. Besides spiced mutton, beef is also prized. Both kinds of meat are often served in the form of soups to which potatoes or noodles are added. Another common dish is made from pieces of meat that have been left on the bone and are served

with a broth flavored with salt and onions. Shoulder of mutton is considered particularly tasty; after it has

been eaten, the bones are used as an oracle. The fat from the tail of a sheep and boiled camel meat are al-

so among the favorite delicacies. Bodoog is also very popular: to make this, the almost intact skin of a goat, from which all bones and innards have been removed, is filled with seasoned pieces of meat and red-hot stones. Then the "animal bag" is tied up so that it is airtight and roasted from the outside; in this way that the meat is braised from all sides in its own juice and becomes marvelously tender.

Anyone who enters a Mongolian yurt of the inhabitants of the steppe will be welcomed with a bowl of brick tea that the nomads make from pressed tea bricks with salt and fatty milk. In the north of the Gobi, slightly sour flakes of dried skin of the milk often float on this brew. They serve *boorsog* with the tea: small cakes deep-fried in fat. Airag (fermented, alcoholic mare's milk) is the national drink and has a special symbolic value. This is because of the white color of the milk, representing purity, and, furthermore, the gods are believed to be involved in the fermentation process.

extremely hot in summer. In the heart of the desert regions, temperatures between 30 and 45 degrees Celsius (86-113o F) are normal, while in Ulan Bator, maximum summer temperatures are around 37 degrees Celsius (99o F). Sharp drops in temperature (particularly at night) occur almost everywhere in Mongolia from October onwards. Spring, in contrast, is characterized by rapid increases in temperature, although snowfall or precipitation in the form of rain or showers also occurs frequently.

Passports and Visas

To travel to Mongolia, visitors need a passport that is valid for at least a further six months, a passport photograph, and a completed application form for a visa (available from Mongolian embassies). Tourists must be able to

prove they have reserved a return journey; if they wish to travel as a transit passenger through Mongolia, the connecting ticket will be required. As visa regulations have been altered frequently in recent years, it is advisable to contact the Mongolian embassies for information:

Embassy of Mongolia, Washington D.C.
Address: Embassy of Mongolia, 2833 M Street NW Washington, DC, 20007
Hours of operation: Monday-Friday 09:00-13:00 and 14:00-17:00
Telephone: (202)-333 7117, Fax: (202)-298 9227

E-mail: esyam@mongolianembassy.us
www.mongolianembassy.us
Embassy of Mongolia in the United Kingdom
Embassy of Mongolia: 7 Kensington Court London W8 5DL

Telephone: +44 (0) 20 7937 0150,
Fax: +44 (0) 20 7937 1117
E-mail:
office@embassyofmongolia.co.uk
www.embassyofmongolia.co.uk

Time Zones

The time difference to England during winter (GMT) is plus 8 hours (in summer: BST plus 7 hours). During winter time the difference to New York is minus 11 hours and to Los Angeles, minus 8 hours. Since 1999, changing the clocks for winter and summer time has been abolished in Mongolia, as the majority of Mongolians, especially those outside the larger cities, did not find it to be of any benefit or relevance.

Getting There

Chinggis Khaan International Airport (IATA: ULN, ICAO: ZMUB) is the international airport serving Ulan Bator, Mongolia. It is the largest international air facility in the country, and the only facility to offer scheduled international flights. The airport is the main base of operations for national carriers MIAT Mongolian Airlines and Aero Mongolia; the Mongolian national airline, MIAT – Mongolian International Air Transport (OM) (www.miat.com) has flights all year round to Berlin, Moscow, Beijing, and Seoul, and in the summer months to Osaka and Tokyo. Other airlines that serve Mongolia are: Aeroflot (suitable for travelers from Europe, via Moscow), Korean Air (useful for North Americans, via

In the Altai Mountains, it is often necessary to rely on help from someone with local knowledge (top, left and right). – Travelers in Mongolia enjoy a picnic in the open air (bottom). Ulan Bator: using an umbrella as a sunshade (eight-hand page, top). Tour group at a gas station in the Khangai Mountains (right-hand page, bottom).

Where Nature Becomes an Adventure

Traveling in the Land of the Nomads

Experiencing the wilderness of Mongolia from a canoe on the lake Khurgan Nuur. (1) or when camping in the snow-covered Altai Mountains (2).

The land of the descendants of Genghis Khan is not only a land with a magnificent culture transcending time, where many nomads have remained faithful to their ancient customs; it is also a land of adventure with seemingly endless open spaces, where a traveler can experience many things that would not be possible to the same extent in Western countries. In a seemingly endless region of primeval nature, one can experience breathtaking landscapes: rugged mountain ranges, basalt volcanic cones, raging rivers, watery plateaus strewn with lakes, and the sand fields of the desert. More still: here in the midst of entrancing scenery, far from all towns, villages and oases, the most adventurous dreams that perhaps have been floating around in your head for a long, long time, become reality – riding on a Mongolian horse through the steppe; sleeping in an isolated yurt or sitting at a camp fire on a starry night.

Mongolia offers every visitor an endless abundance of genuine experiences of nature, whether as a hiker, climber or canoeist. Those who want to discover the wilderness will find it in the natural open spaces of Mongolia, and every traveler can choose how to get around – by horse, camel, mountain bike, motor cycle, or jeep. At the same time, it must be emphasized that for traveling in the steppe, taiga or desert, in the mountains or in the forests, on the rivers or lakes, one must be in the best of health, both physically and mentally. Over-estimating one's own reserves for many non-conformist ventures in Mongolia is completely misguided. Instead, patience, skill in improvisation, endurance and the ability to find one's bearings in unfamiliar surroundings are important qualifica-

a kayak – seeing Mongolia from a completely new perspective. The frequent contrasts between fast flowing rivers and peaceful lakes is particularly delightful. One can follow gently flowing streams and then plough through foaming torrents, such as those of the Khovd Gol, the largest river of the Mongolian Altai. And as one drifts downriver, wind-proofed yurts, grazing yaks or green carpets of steppe grass with thousands of edelweiss glide past.

4

tions for a tour through the wilderness. For example, if you visit the former empire of Genghis Khan to do some mountain climbing, you will find no shortage of gigantic mountain ranges and volcanoes with alpine conditions, but in all regions you must expect sudden changes in the weather. Even in summer, some regions can be hit by severe cold spells or snowfall. And if you wish to travel on the back of a "ship of the desert" in the realm of the Gobi you must take plenty of food and drinking water, in order not to become a victim of the aridity and lack of water.

In the imposing scenery of Mon-

golia, no limits are set to the thirst for adventure of mountain bikers or motor cyclists. But, as a result of the extreme climatic conditions and break-neck trails, progress can sometimes be quite arduous. So, cyclists should plan appropriately, setting modest daily targets.

If you mainly want to explore Mongolia with a jeep or off-road vehicle, these are available for rental at the bus station in Ulan Bator. As there is barely any difference in the prices for a vehicle with or without a driver, it is a good idea to take someone with you who knows the country. Outside Ulan Bator, the roads in Mon-

5

golia are extremely poor and covered in potholes and frost damage.

A memorable experience can also take the form of a trip on a river, following one of the many watercourses and – seated in a canoe or

When traveling with a backpack, one must frequently wade through bubbling mountain streams (3 and 5), where the chances of hooking a trout for dinner are pretty high. (4).

153

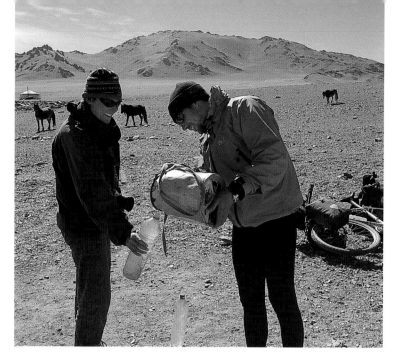

Cyclists need large quantities of water in the Altai Mountains (above).

Curious Mongolian children examine the cameras of the visitors (below).

Information

For those interested in traveling to Mongolia, the home pages of the various Mongolian embassies provide information about visa regulations. Regarding safety issues when traveling, the US State Department or the British Foreign and Com-monwealth Office or the equivalent in your country should be contacted. General or current information, for example, exchange rates, weather forecasts etc. can be found at the web site: ulaanbaatar.net and cultural information at www.mongoliatoday.com or from the Arts Council of Mongolia: tel./fax: 976-11-319015, e-mail: artscouncil@magicnet.mn.

Getting Around Within the Country

There are a number of ways of getting around in Mongolia. Tourists can make use of regular scheduled and long-distance buses that serve the main towns of all the aimags (provinces). Fares are very much cheaper than bus trips operated by tourist travel enterprises. In addition, there are Russian vans (for about 10 passengers) that leave from the bus station in Ulan Bator, about 300 meters (328 yards) east of the central train station.

Those who are interested in rail travel should not hesitate to use the extremely cheap "wood class" on the train, i.e. carriages in which the seats consist of wooden benches. In this manner, one can rattle from the Russian to the Chinese border, or make excursions and trips to Erdenet, Darkhan, or Dsamyn-Uud. In the summer months, a so-called tourist train runs from the north of Mongolia to Erlian in China. Information can be obtained from the Mongolian Railway's Tour Bureau: tel.: 00976/11/944458, 943841, fax: 00976/11/944453. Many domestic flights can also be

Seoul) and Air China (good for travelers from Australia and New Zealand).

Hints for Photographers

For a journey through Mongolia, photographic equipment should be as light and as flexible as possible, while still meeting the wishes of the photographer with regard to his motifs. Lovers of plants and animals will not be able to do without a large zoom lens. All equipment should be packed for good protection from dust, moisture and shocks.

The light conditions in Mongolia (clear air and strong ultraviolet radiation) mean that UV and skylight filters are a must. They reduce over-dominant blue tones and protect the lens. Because of the intensity of the light (above all in the Gobi Desert), slow film speeds are especially suitable.

The strong wind often makes shorter shutter speeds a necessity, at the cost of depth of field. Taking pictures of police, military and airport complexes is not permitted in Mongolia. Regulations regarding photography in museums or at religious sites should also be strictly observed. If you still wish to take a photograph, be sure to ask permission first; occasionally you may also have to pay a small fee.

booked in Mongolia, for example, with the Mongolian airline MIAT (tel.: 00976/11/379935, 984070, fax: 00976/11/379919, www.miat.com) or with Blue Sky Aviation (tel.: 00976/11/312085, fax: 00976/11/322857), an airline in Ulan Bator, that uses modern, western aircraft and, like MIAT, offers flights to all the provincial capitals. Furthermore, sightseeing flights in biplanes or helicopter flights to remote regions are available. Other means of transport in the country are, according to preference, motor cycle, mountain bike, canoe, kayak or camel and horse. Hitch-hiking is not recommended in Mongolia, since, as a method of transport for foreigners, it is completely unknown. The likelihood of finding a ride is extremely small.

Health Precautions

Immunizations are not obligatory for a visit to Mongolia. Nevertheless, it is strongly recommended that tetanus and polio vaccinations should be renewed. Protection against hepatitis A, immunization against diphtheria and cholera prophylaxis are also advisable, as in 1996 the first cases of cholera in Mongolia were observed. A remark on the current situation: there have been several cases of the new virus disease, SARS in Ulan Bator.
In emergencies or in the case of serious illness, one should contact the medical emergency service. The number for the entire coun-

try is 103. Furthermore, one can call the Mongolian First Assistance, where the telephones are available round the clock: tel. 311801, 326939 and mobile: 99114848, 99190038, 99191881).

Accommodation

In the larger towns and cities of Mongolia there are plenty of hotels and guest houses in a range of categories. Furnished rooms and apartments can also be rented from private owners. Outside Ulan Bator, Darkhan and Erdenet, however, there are very few hotels that could be recommended. And in the thinly populated areas, where yurts are the main form of accommodation, one should, if at all possible, bring a sleeping bag – as well as soap, toilet roll and a towel.
The customary hospitality of nomadic Mongolians is occasionally

Cyclists touring in the land of the Mongols will sometimes come across simple signs in the wide expanses of steppe, that advertise overnight accommodation in yurts.

expressed in the offer of their own yurt as guest accommodation, while the family then moves in with the neighbors. If one is shown an honor of this kind when in the country, the host should be offered a little money or snuff as a gift; the lady of the "house" will appreciate a nicely-scented bar of soap and the children will be delighted with some candy. Accommodation is seldom available in the more remote small towns, villages and oases. Everyone traveling in Mongolia should therefore have a waterproof and weather-resistant tent in their luggage; in this way, one remains independent and can avoid much trouble in the hotels, many of which are extremely run down.

Public Holidays and Religious Festivals

Some of the most important public holidays are January 1, when Mongolians celebrate New Year, and Independence Day, celebrated on November 26. In addition, there is the three-day-long festival of the new moon (Tsagaan-Sar) between the end of January and mid-February. The exact date of the festival, which is strongly influenced by animistic elements, is determined by the Buddhist lunar calendar. The most famous festival of the Mongolians is the Nadaam Festival. It takes place each year from July 11–13.

Currency

The national currency is the freely convertible tugrik (MNT). 1 tugrik = 100 mongo. The second legal means of payment is the US dollar.

With Horse-head Fiddle and Human Larynx

The Traditional Music of the Mongols

An essential feature of traditional Mongolian music is the use of wind and plucked instruments: Jew's harp, kettledrums and violins with several strings. In particular, the horse-head fiddle (in Mongolian: morin khuur), which is exclusively played by men, is popular everywhere in the country. This is a two-stringed viola da gamba with a head carved in the shape of a horse's head and strings made of horse-hair, giving the instrument a unique sound. When Mongolian musicians play it, they create a music that echoes the vast ocean of the steppe in a remarkable manner.

Many Mongolian songs sound strange to European ears and may appear monotonous. This is also true of overtone singing – a special type of singing in Mongolia. This is achieved with enormous strain on larynx, vocal chords and diaphragm, as the singer produces a low basic tone and, simultaneously, a second, very much higher melody, the so-called overtone, which overrides the basic tone. In Mongolia, the epic singers are also highly esteemed; they perform folk tales handed down in the oral tradition. These tell of love, of nature and the great heroes of the nomads. Gifted singers skillfully match the emotional melodies to the rhyming of the epic poem. On long winter evenings, the recitations of the epic singers and their melodies are a welcome form of entertainment in the yurts.

1

2

3

4

Besides various kinds of stringed and plucked instruments (1), the two-stringed horse-head fiddle (morin khuur) is the most important musical instrument in Mongolia (2 and 3) and is used at the national circus as well as in the most simple yurt, where one sometimes will also meet an accordion player (4).

According to an old tradition, the morin khuur may be played only by men. It has strings made from horse-hair (right-hand page).

156

People,
Places and Topics

Mongolian family in the Khangai Mountains.

Evening mood at the lake Khar Nuur in the Altai Mountains.

Magnificent scenery in the Altai.

Texts and Picture Credits / Imprint

The Photographer

Since his youth, Olaf Meinhardt has traveled throughout the world on foot and by bicycle. A journey around the world by bicycle was the beginning of his career as a photographer. His reports of previous trips to Mongolia and South America in have been published in photographic journals and books..

The Author

Achill Moser, born in 1954, studied African Studies, Arabic and Economics. Since 1979 he has worked as a freelance journalist, photographer, author of books and speaker. His travel reports have appeared in the magazines GEO and STERN. He has also appeared in many television broadcasts and has published more than 20 books.

On many extensive trips, he has made frequent visits to both China and Mongolia.

Furthermore, he has undertaken more than 30 expeditions, adding up to a total of five years – on foot and by camel through 25 deserts of the world. Like a nomad, he followed the forgotten caravan trails, ancient paths of pilgrims and the routes taken by historical explorers. His motto is: "To walk through the deserts of the world, at a speed that the soul can keep in step with …"

Achill Moser took the photographs for the chapter "Where the Son of the Blue Wolf Rests – With Camels and on Foot Through Inner Mongolia."

Cover photographs:
Front cover: In the Altai Mountains
Back cover: Nomadic child with goats.

Page 1: A yurt with heating
Page 3: Mongolian child wearing traditional cap with a conical tip. Exotically-shaped stupas at the Lamaist monastery of Erdene Zuu.

Text Credits

We would like to express our gratitude to all copyright owners for their kind permission to reprint texts from:

"Im Land der zornigen Winde" (In the Land of the Angry Winds) by Galsan Tschinag and Amélie Schenk, Zürich 1999. (p. 10)

"The Mission of Friar William of Rubruck. His Journey to the Court of the Great Khan Mongke 1253-1255", translated by Jackson, Peter and David Morgan, London 1990 (Quote from p. 58, 69)

"Geheime Geschichte der Mongolen" (The secret history of the Mongolian people) by Manfred Taube, Munich 1989.

"Die Karawane" (The Caravan, story) in »Mein Altai« by Galsan Tschinag, Munich 2005. (Quote from p. 12, 40)

"Tibet: Land of Snows" by Giuseppe Tucci, Paul Elek, London 1973. (Quote from p. 80)

"Across the Gobi Desert"by Sven Hedin, Lonon 1933. (Quote from p. 102, 108)

"Il Milione – Die Wunder der Welt" (The wonders of the world) by Marco Polo, Zürich 1986. (Quotes from p. 39, 115, 121)

"Mit Sven Hedin durch Asiens Wüsten" (With Sven Hedin Across the Deserts of Asia) by Paul Lieberenz and Dr. Arthur Berger, Berlin 1932. (Quotes from p. 122, 134)

Picture Credits

Achill Moser, Hamburg: pp. 5 Center L and bottom R; p. 111 top R, pp. 122 (3), 123, 124 (3), 125 (2), 126 (7), 127, 128/129, 132/133, 133, 134 (2), 134/135, 137.

Archiv für Kunst und Geschichte, Berlin: pp. 18l., 19 (2), 38, 39 (2), 120 (2), 121; Picture-Alliance/akg-images, Frankfurt: p. 27 bottom R.

All other pictures are by Olaf Meinhardt, Braunschweig.

We would like to thank all copyright owners and publishers for their permission to reprint and publish. In spite of intensive efforts, it has not been possible to establish all copyright owners. We would kindly request these to contact us.

This work has been carefully researched by the author and kept up to date as well as checked by the publisher for coherence. However, the publishing house can assume no liability for the accuracy of the data contained herein.

We are always grateful for suggestions and advice. Please send your comments to:
C.J. Bucher Publishing,
Product Management
Innsbrucker Ring 15
81673 Munich
Germany
E-mail:
editorial@bucher-publishing.com
Homepage:
www.bucher-publishing.com

Imprint

Translation:
Janet Mayer, Bruchsal, Germany
Proofreading:
Jane Michael, Munich, Germany
Cartography: Astrid Fischer-Leitl, Munich, Germany

Product management for the German edition: Joachim Hellmuth
Product management for the English edition: Dr. Birgit Kneip
Graphic Design: BuchHaus Robert Gigler GmbH, Munich, Germany, revised by Agnes Meyer-Wilmes, Munich, Germany
Production: Bettina Schippel
Repro: Repro Ludwig, Zell am See, Austria
Printed in Slovenia by MKT Print, Ljubljana

See our full listing of books at
www.bucher-publishing.com